Collins
revision guides

TotalRevision

GCSE French

■ **Dave Carter**

■ **Series editor: Jayne de Courcy**

Published by HarperCollins*Publishers* Ltd
77-85 Fulham Palace Road
London W6 8JB

www.CollinsEducation.com
On-line support for schools and colleges

© HarperCollins*Publishers* 2003

First published 2001
This new edition published 2003
10 9 8 7 6 5 4 3 2
ISBN 0 00 713620 X

British Library Cataloguing in Publication Data
A catalogue record for this book is available from the British Library.

Edited by Jenny Draine
Production by Jack Murphy
Series design by Sally Boothroyd
Index compiled by Yvonne Dixon
Book design by Ken Vail Graphic Design, Cambridge
Printed and bound in China by Imago

Acknowledgements
The Author and Publishers are grateful to the following for permission to reproduce copyright material:

Photographs
Tim Booth Title page, 40, 65, 73
Telegraph Colour Library Title page, 25, 55, 71
Travel Ink Title page, 37, 67

Illustrations
Kathy Baxendale; Richard Deverell; Hilary Evans; Gecko Ltd; Sarah Jowsey; Dave Poole; Nick Ward

Every effort has been made to contact the holders of copyright material, but if any have been inadvertently overlooked, the Publishers will be pleased to make the necessary arrangements at the first opportunity.

Audio CD
The audio CD was recorded at Post Sound Studios, London and was produced by the Language Production Company with the voices of Jérôme Ambroggi, Laetitia Ambroggi, Jean-Pierre Blanchard, Juliet Dante, Alexandre Pageon, Katherine Pageon, Sarah Sherborne.

Production by Marie-Thérèse Bougard and Charlie Waygood.

Music by Nigel Martinez and Dick Walter.

You might also like to visit:

www.fireandwater.com
The book lover's website

CONTENTS AND REVISION PLANNER

	On syllabus	Revise again	Revised & understood

UNIT 1 L'ECOLE SCHOOL
Revision Session 1: What you need to know — 1
2: Higher vocabulary — 3
3: How the grammar works — 5

UNIT 2 A LA MAISON/LES MEDIA HOME LIFE AND MEDIA
Revision Session 1: What you need to know — 7
2: Higher vocabulary — 9
3: How the grammar works — 10

UNIT 3 LA SANTE, LA FORME ET LA NOURRITURE HEALTH, FITNESS AND FOOD
Revision Session 1: What you need to know — 13
2: Higher vocabulary — 15
3: How the grammar works — 16

UNIT 4 MOI, MA FAMILLE ET MES AMIS SELF, FAMILY AND FRIENDS
Revision Session 1: What you need to know — 19
2: Higher vocabulary — 21
3: How the grammar works — 22

UNIT 5 LE TEMPS LIBRE, LES LOISIRS, LES VACANCES ET LES FETES FREE TIME, LEISURE, HOLIDAYS AND SPECIAL OCCASIONS
Revision Session 1: What you need to know — 23
2: Higher vocabulary — 25
3: How the grammar works — 26

UNIT 6 LES RAPPORTS PERSONNELS, LES ACTIVITES SOCIALES ET LES RENDEZ-VOUS PERSONAL RELATIONSHIPS, SOCIAL ACTIVITIES AND MEETINGS
Revision Session 1: What you need to know — 29
2: Higher vocabulary — 31
3: How the grammar works — 32

UNIT 7 LA VILLE, LES REGIONS ET LE TEMPS HOME TOWN, LOCAL ENVIRONMENT AND WEATHER
Revision Session 1: What you need to know — 35
2: Higher vocabulary — 37
3: How the grammar works — 38

UNIT 8 LES COURSES ET LES SERVICES PUBLICS SHOPPING AND PUBLIC SERVICES
Revision Session 1: What you need to know — 40
2: Higher vocabulary — 42
3: How the grammar works — 43

UNIT 9 LA ROUTE, LES VOYAGES ET LES TRANSPORTS FINDING THE WAY, GETTING AROUND, TRAVEL AND TRANSPORT
Revision Session 1: What you need to know — 46
2: Higher vocabulary — 48
3: How the grammar works — 50

UNIT 10 L'ENSEIGNEMENT SUPERIEUR, LA FORMATION ET L'EMPLOI
          FURTHER EDUCATION, TRAINING AND JOBS
Revision Session 1: What you need to know   53
               2: Higher vocabulary   55
               3: How the grammar works   57

UNIT 11 LA PUBLICITE, LES COMMUNICATIONS ET LES LANGUES
          AU TRAVAIL ADVERTISING, COMMUNICATION AND
          LANGUAGES AT WORK
Revision Session 1: What you need to know   59
               2: Higher vocabulary   61
               3: How the grammar works   63

UNIT 12 LA VIE A L'ETRANGER, LE TOURISME, LES COUTUMES ET
          LE LOGEMENT CUSTOMS AND ACCOMMODATION
Revision Session 1: What you need to know   65
               2: Higher vocabulary   67
               3: How the grammar works   69

UNIT 13 LE MONDE THE WORLD
Revision Session 1: What you need to know   71
               2: Higher vocabulary   73
               3: How the grammar works   75

UNIT 14 EXAM PRACTICE LISTENING AND RESPONDING
Revision Session 1: How to overcome problems   77
               2: Points to practise   80
               3: Higher Level performance   83
               4: Different kinds of listening   85
               5: Different kinds of question   87
               6: Questions to try   90

UNIT 15 EXAM PRACTICE SPEAKING
Revision Session 1: How to overcome problems   92
               2: Hints on pronunciation   95
               3: How to tackle role-plays   98
               4: How to tackle Presentation and Discussion 100
               5: How to tackle General Conversation   102
               6: Questions to try   104

UNIT 16 EXAM PRACTICE READING AND RESPONDING
Revision Session 1: How to overcome problems   108
               2: Higher Level performance   112
               3: Different kinds of reading   114
               4: Different kinds of question   117
               5: Questions to try   119

UNIT 17 EXAM PRACTICE WRITING
Revision Session 1: How to overcome problems   124
               2: Different kinds of question   127
               3: Different kinds of writing   129
               4: Higher Level performance   130
               5: Questions to try   132

On syllabus	Revise again	Revised & understood

UNIT 18 FURTHER GRAMMAR

Possessive pronouns 137
Intensifiers 137
Position of pronouns 138
Relative pronouns 138
Prepositions 139
Conjunctions 140
Irregular verbs 140
Impersonal verbs 143
The future perfect tense 143
The conditional perfect tense 144
The past historic tense 144
The subjunctive 144
List of common verbs 145

CHECK YOURSELF ANSWERS 145
ANSWERS AND TRANSCRIPTS FOR QUESTIONS TO TRY 163

INDEX 180

GRAMMAR FINDER

Most aspects of grammar are covered in the 13 topic units, but aspects not dealt with in the topic units are covered in the Further grammar section in Unit 18. The chart below shows you all the grammar that is covered in this book and where you will be able to find it.

	UNIT NUMBER(S)	PAGE NUMBER(S)
Nouns	3	16
Articles	3	17
Adjectives	4	22
Comparison of	7	38
Demonstrative	11	64
Indefinite	13	75–6
Possessive	4	22
Superlative of	11	63
Intensifiers	18	137–8
Adverbs	8	45
Comparison of	7	38
Indefinite	13	75–6
Superlative of	11	63
Intensifiers	18	137–8
Pronouns		
Demonstrative	11	64
Emphatic	6, 13	34, 75
Indefinite	13	75–6
Object	6, 13	32–3, 75
Position of	6, 18	33–4, 138
Possessive	18	137
Relative	6, 13, 18	33–4, 75, 138–9
Subject	6, 13	32
Prepositions	18	139–40
Conjunctions	18	140

	UNIT NUMBER(S)	PAGE NUMBER(S)
Negatives	10	57–8
Interrogatives	9	50–51
Number and time		
Dates	1	5
Numbers	8	43–4
Quantities	8	44
Time	1, 12	5–6, 70
Verbs		
Common	18	145–7
Impersonal	18	143
Irregular	2, 18	12, 140–43
Reflexive	2, 5	11, 28
Conditional perfect tense	18	144
Conditional tense	7	39
Future perfect tense	18	143
Future tense	7	38–9
Imperative (commands)	1	6
Imperfect tense	12	69
Infinitive	5	26
Passive	10	58
Past historic tense	18	144
Perfect tense	5	27–8
Pluperfect tense	12	69–70
Present participle	3	18
Present tense	2	10–11
Subjunctive	18	144–5

ABOUT THIS BOOK

This book has been structured to help you revise **effectively** and **confidently** for your GCSE French exam:

- **Vocabulary and grammar revision** has been broken down into a number of short revision sessions
- Quick Check yourself questions **test your understanding** and **pinpoint any weaknesses**
- **Higher Level** material is clearly highlighted for **ease of revision**
- Separate revision sessions cover the **four skill areas** (Listening, Speaking, Reading and Writing) to **improve your exam technique**
- Questions to try give you further practice in answering **typical exam questions** in Listening, Speaking, Reading and Writing.

Vocabulary and grammar revision sessions

The **vocabulary** you need to know is broken down into 13 topic units. Within each topic, the vocabulary is further divided into two short revision sessions called What you need to know and Higher vocabulary (see 'Foundation and Higher Level material' opposite). You should be able to read through each of these in no more than **15–20 minutes**. That is the maximum amount of time that you should spend on revising without taking a short break.

The **grammar** you need to know is also broken up into short revision sessions called How the grammar works. Any grammar not covered within Units 1–13 can be found in the Further grammar section on pages 137–47, which includes a useful list of all the common verbs you will need to know. The Grammar finder chart on pages vi and vii should help you to find any aspect of grammar quickly and easily.

Check yourself questions

At the end of each topic revision session there are a number of Check yourself questions. When you try to answer these, you will immediately find out whether you have **remembered** and **understood** what you have read in the revision session. All the answers are provided at the back of the book (on pages 148–62), along with helpful advice and tips on how to avoid common mistakes.

If you manage to answer all the Check yourself questions for a session correctly, then you can confidently tick off this topic in the box provided in the Contents and revision planner. If many of your answers are incorrect, then you will need to tick the 'Revise again' box to remind yourself to return to this topic later in your revision programme.

✎ Foundation and Higher Level material

You will find everything you need in this book, whether you are revising for the **Foundation Tier** or the **Higher Tier** French exam.

Vocabulary that is only needed for the Higher Tier is separated out in the Higher vocabulary topic revision sessions. Any grammar that only applies to Higher Tier is also clearly indicated by a **green background** and an appropriate stamp in the margin (see right).

✎ Improving your exam technique

Four Exam practice units (Units 14–17) focus on the **four skill areas** you will be examined on in your French exam: Listening, Speaking, Reading and Writing.

The author, who is an experienced examiner, explains the **types of questions** you will meet, how to **overcome potential problems** and how to ensure that you perform as well as you possibly can in your exams.

✎ Questions to try

You are also given the opportunity to answer **typical exam questions** on the four skill areas in the Questions to try sections, which you will find at the end of the Exam practice units. The **CD** also ensures that you have lots of practice for your **Listening exam**.

Answers are given at the back of the book (on pages 163–79) against which you can **compare your own answers**. There are also Examiner's comments showing what you need to do to score **high marks** when answering questions in your GCSE French exams, as well as full transcripts for all the recorded material.

Working through the skills revision sessions will give you an **excellent grounding in exam technique**. If you feel you need even more exam practice, then this can be found in *Do Brilliantly GCSE French*, also published by Collins Educational.

About your GCSE French course

✐ Awarding bodies

- This guide has been produced to help you study and revise for the French exams set by the GCSE awarding bodies of England (AQA [Specifications A and B], Edexcel and OCR) from 2003 onwards.

- Although this guide was written to cover the requirements of all the awarding bodies, it is important that you know the exact requirements of your own exam, particularly the length of the different tests, the nature of the Speaking Test and the rules for Coursework.

✐ Grammar

- The grammatical content of all the GCSE specifications is the same, and is covered in the How the grammar works sections of this book as well as in the Further Grammar section (mainly Higher Level) in Unit 18. The Check yourself questions will help you to practise the use of the relevant grammar points.

✐ Vocabulary

- The core vocabulary printed in the specifications is different for each awarding body, as is the amount of guidance given about Higher Tier vocabulary. No guide can give a comprehensive list of all the words which may appear in any exam paper; however, if you know all the vocabulary in this guide, you are unlikely to come across many unknown words in your exam. However, one of the higher level skills is the ability to deal with words you haven't met before, so the more you know about language patterns in French, and similarities between French and English, the better you'll be able to cope. **You will not be able to refer to a dictionary in any part of the exam, except for Coursework.**

✐ Types of questions

- The Exam practice units include Questions to try, which are examples of the types of questions used by the different awarding bodies. In Listening and Reading, the question types used by the awarding bodies are very similar, and all the questions in this guide will be helpful whichever exam you are doing. The Writing and Speaking questions will also be of value, but a note is included to tell you which are most appropriate for your particular exam.

- All Speaking Tests involve Role-plays (for Edexcel and OCR these include a Foundation/Higher Role-play done by both Foundation **and** Higher candidates) and a conversation. AQA and OCR also include a prepared Presentation.

✐ Foundation and Higher Tiers

- You will have to decide (in consultation with your teacher) which Tier of each test you will take. You can take a combination (for example, Foundation Writing and Listening, with Higher Reading and Speaking). If you take all four Foundation tests, you can reach a maximum Grade C. If you take two Foundation and two Higher tests, you **could** reach Grade A (and Grade B with three Foundation and only one Higher), but you would have to score **very** high marks in each test to do so. To get an A* you have to do all four Higher tests.

UNIT 1: L'ECOLE
SCHOOL

REVISION SESSION 1 — What you need to know

Levez-vous.	Stand up.
Asseyez-vous.	Sit down.
Ouvrez la fenêtre/vos cahiers.	Open the window/your exercise books.
Fermez la porte/le livre.	Close the door/the book.
Taisez-vous.	Be quiet.
Je (ne) comprends (pas).	I (don't) understand.
Pouvez-vous répéter, s'il vous plaît?	Can you say it again, please?

Mon école est très grande.	My school is very large.
Il y a mille cinq cents élèves.	There are 1,500 pupils.
Il y a beaucoup de salles de classe.	There are lots of classrooms.
Il n'y a pas de laboratoire de langues.	There is no language laboratory.
La rentrée, c'est le mardi deux septembre.	We go back to school on Tuesday 2nd September.
Les grandes vacances commencent le 23 juillet.	The summer holidays start on 23rd July.
On est en vacances du 8 au 12 février.	We are on holiday from the 8th to the 12th February.

Le premier cours commence à neuf heures vingt.	The first lesson begins at 9.20.
Il y a une récréation de 10h20 à 10h45.	There is a break from 10.20 to 10.45.
Le déjeuner est à midi vingt.	Lunch is at 12.20.
Je mange à la cantine.	I eat in the canteen/dining hall.
Chaque cours dure quarante minutes.	Each lesson lasts for 40 minutes.
Les cours finissent à 3h30.	Lessons finish at 3.30.
Le soir, j'ai deux heures de devoirs.	In the evening, I have two hours' homework.
Le mercredi, je n'ai pas cours.	I don't have school on Wednesdays.

Je viens au collège à pied.	I walk to school.
Je suis membre du club de gym.	I'm a member of the gym club.
L'uniforme scolaire est affreux.	The school uniform is awful.
Je porte une jupe grise.	I wear a grey skirt.
Les garçons portent une cravate/un pantalon.	The boys wear a tie/trousers.
Je fais partie de l'équipe d'athlétisme.	I'm in the athletics team.
Je suis en seconde.	I'm in Year 11.
Mon frère est en quatrième.	My brother is in Year 9.

Je fais de l'histoire, de l'EMT…	I do History, Design Technology…
Ma matière préférée, c'est la physique.	My favourite subject is Physics.
Le prof d'anglais s'appelle M. Martin.	The English teacher is called Mr Martin.
Je n'aime pas le professeur de gymnastique.	I don't like the gym teacher.
Je suis bon(ne) en espagnol.	I'm good at Spanish.
Je parle bien l'allemand.	I speak German well.
Je suis nul(le) en sciences.	I'm useless at Science.
J'ai de bonnes notes.	I get good marks.
La technologie, c'est facile.	Technology is easy.

LES MOIS

janvier	juillet
février	août
mars	septembre
avril	octobre
mai	novembre
juin	décembre

DES ADJECTIFS

intelligent	intelligent
stupide	stupid
bête	silly
fort en	good at
doué	clever
amusant	amusing/funny
difficile	difficult
facile	easy
passionnant	fascinating
intéressant	interesting
ennuyeux/euse	boring
fatigant	tiring
utile	useful
inutile	useless

QUESTIONS UTILES

Comment ça s'écrit?	How do you spell it?
Comment dit-on X en français?	How do you say X in French?
C'est quoi en français?	What is it in French?
Qu'est-ce que ça veut dire?	What does that mean?

LES MATIERES

 l'anglais   le français   la chimie   la physique   la biologie

 l'EPS (le sport)   la musique   le dessin   les mathématiques   la géographie

 l'espagnol   l'informatique   l'histoire   l'EMT (la technologie)

QUAND?

le matin	in the morning
l'après-midi	in the afternoon
le soir	in the evening
par jour	per day
par semaine	per week
jeudi	on Thursday
le dimanche	on Sundays

QUESTIONS/PROMPTS

Parlez-moi de votre école.
Les cours commencent à quelle heure?
C'est quand, les vacances de Noël?
Décrivez votre uniforme.
Vous êtes en quelle classe?
Quelle est votre matière préférée?
Vous êtes membre d'un club?

? CHECK YOURSELF QUESTIONS

Q1 How would you say this in French?

A My favourite subject is Maths.
B On Wednesdays, lessons begin at 9.45.
C My sister is in Year 7.
D I like the Science teacher.
E There are a lot of pupils at my school.

Q2 C'est quelle matière?

A On utilise des ordinateurs.
B Langue parlée à Berlin.
C On étudie les plantes.
D On fait beaucoup d'activités sportives.
E On apprend beaucoup de dates.

Answers are on page 148.

Higher vocabulary

A L'ECOLE

sixième	Year 7
cinquième	Year 8
quatrième	Year 9
troisième	Year 10
seconde	Year 11
première	Year 12
terminale	Year 13
le bac(calauréat)	exam taken at end of *terminale*

QUELLE ECOLE?

le collège	school (Years 7–10)
le lycée	school (Years 11–13)
une école mixte	a mixed school
une école de filles	a girls' school
une école publique	a state school
une école privée	a private school
un(e) pensionnaire	a boarder
un(e) demi-pensionnaire	a half-boarder (stays at school for lunch)

Je déteste les maths parce que c'est trop difficile.	I hate Maths because it's too difficult.
Je ne suis pas bon(ne) élève, car je ne travaille pas assez.	I'm not a good student, because I don't work hard enough.
J'attends les grandes vacances avec impatience.	I can't wait for the summer holidays.
J'espère réussir au bac l'année prochaine.	I hope to pass the 'bac' next year.
Je ne supporte vraiment pas l'école.	I really can't stand school.
Les profs me critiquent toujours.	The teachers are always criticising me.
Je voudrais bien apprendre d'autres langues.	I'd love to learn (some) other languages.
J'apprends le français depuis cinq ans.	I've been learning French for five years.
L'année passée je n'ai pas travaillé, mais maintenant je fais des progrès.	Last year I didn't work, but now I'm making progress.
Je préfère les écoles mixtes parce que ça ressemble plus à la vie normale.	I prefer mixed schools because they're more like real life.
J'ai choisi ce collège car il est près de chez moi.	I chose this school because it's near where I live.
Je suis pensionnaire, parce que j'habite loin du lycée.	I'm a boarder because I live a long way from school.

You can make even quite simple statements earn extra marks for Higher Level, by adding extra information:

- Say how long you've been doing something:
  J'étudie l'italien depuis deux ans.

- Express opinions and give a reason:
  J'aime le prof de maths, car il est très sympa.

- Say why you do/have done something:
  Je fais des sciences parce que c'est une matière passionnante.

EXTRA DETAILS

mais	but
et	and
puis	then
donc	therefore
alors	so
car	for
parce que	because
à cause de	because of
malgré	in spite of

- Use linking words to avoid a series of very short sentences:
  Je suis intelligente. Je ne travaille pas assez. → *Je suis intelligente mais je ne travaille pas assez.*

- To make a change from *car* or *parce que* followed by a verb, try another linking phrase:
  J'aime les langues parce que le prof est bon. → *J'aime les langues à cause du prof.*

CHECK YOURSELF QUESTIONS

Q1 How would you say this in French?

A I like Science because I find it interesting.

B I chose English because the teacher is amusing.

C I have been studying Geography for one year.

D I can't stand History because of the homework.

E I'm useless at Music in spite of the good teacher.

Q2 Match the sentence with the right person.

A L'école, ça va. Mais je ne crois pas que je vais réussir à mes examens, car je n'ai pas assez travaillé.

B Je ne supporte pas les profs, et je trouve les cours ennuyeux. Puis on a trop de devoirs.

C Je fais toujours mes devoirs. Tous les soirs, de huit heures à onze heures, je suis dans ma chambre.

Marc, qui n'aime pas l'école
Anne, qui travaille beaucoup
Sandrine, qui n'est pas bonne élève

Answers are on page 148.

How the grammar works

🥖 Dates

- Days and months do not have a capital letter in French. Unlike in English, the date is always expressed in the same way in French, *le* + number + month:

  > *le dix-neuf mars*   March 19th

  An exception is the **1st of the month**, when you use *le premier*:
  > *le premier mai*

- The French do **not** use a word for 'on' with days or dates:

  > *Les cours commencent*   Lessons begin on the 6th of
  > *le six janvier.*   January.
  > *Vendredi, j'ai un examen.*   I have an exam on Friday.

  BUT NOTE:
  > *Je vais à la piscine le jeudi*   I go to the swimming pool on
  >   Thursdays (i.e. every Thursday).

- To use dates to say how long something lasts, use *du* + date + *au* + date:

  > *On est en vacances du trois*   We're on holiday from the 3rd
  >   *au vingt avril.*   to the 20th of April.

🥖 Time

- The time can be expressed very simply in French by using number (hours) + *heures* + number (minutes):

  > *trois heures dix*   3.10/ten past three

  On notices, this will usually be written as *3h10*.
  Remember that *heure* will be singular after *une*:
  > *une heure vingt*

- Other important expressions are:

midi	12 o'clock (midday)
minuit	12 o'clock (midnight)
et quart	quarter past
	(*six heures et quart* – 6.15)
et demie	half past
	(*huit heures et demie* – 8.30)
moins le quart	quarter to
	(*onze heures moins le quart* – 10.45)
moins cinq/dix/vingt/	five/ten/twenty/twenty-five to
vingt-cinq	(*quatre heures moins vingt* – 3.40)

- For timetables, the French always use the **24-hour clock**. So, on a school timetable you might find:
  > *Quatorze heures trente: anglais*   14.30 (2.30pm): English

- To say **what time something happens**, use *à* followed by the time:
  > *J'arrive à l'école à neuf heures*   I get to school at quarter
  >   *moins le quart.*   to nine.

- To indicate **how long something lasts**, you can use *de* with a time, followed by *à* with a later time:

  > *La pause déjeuner est **de** midi*   Lunchtime is from twelve
  > *vingt **à** une heure dix.*   twenty to one ten.

  Or, if you want to avoid a particular time you can use the verb *durer*:

  > *La récréation **dure** vingt minutes.*

- Remember that as well as being used in times, *heure* also means 'hour':

  > *Les cours durent une heure.*

✍ How long for

- To say **how long you have been doing something for**, use *depuis*. It is important to use the right tense, and it's not what you might expect.

- To say how long you **have** been doing something, use *depuis* with the present tense:

  > *Je fais de l'anglais depuis*   I have been doing English for
  > *trois ans.*   three years.

- To say how long you **had** been doing something, use *depuis* with the imperfect tense:

  > *Avant de venir ici, j'étais à l'école*   Before coming here, I had been at
  > *à Paris depuis deux ans.*   school in Paris for two years.

- *Depuis* can also mean 'since':

  > *Je suis là depuis une heure trente.*   I have been here since 1.30.

HIGHER

✍ Commands

- You can often identify when someone is telling you to do something by listening for the *-ez* ending on the verb:

attendez	wait	*écrivez*	write	*finissez*	finish
continuez	continue	*entrez*	come in	*ouvrez*	open
écoutez	listen	*fermez*	close	*prenez*	take

- Remember that if the verb is reflexive, you will also hear the *vous*:

  > *asseyez-vous*   sit down   *levez-vous*   stand up

- If your teacher calls you *tu*, then he/she will simply use the *tu* form of the verb without *tu* (for *er* verbs minus the final *-s*):

  > *attends*   wait   *choisis*   choose   *entre*   come in

- If the verb is reflexive, you will also hear *toi*:

  > *lève-toi*

? CHECK YOURSELF QUESTIONS

Q1 How would you say this in French?

    A the first of August
    B at a quarter to two

C from 3.20 to 4.10
D I've been doing German for five years.
E Look at the board!

Answers are on page 148.

REVISION SESSION I ━━ What you need to know ━━

J'habite une petite maison.	I live in a small house.
Tu habites près du collège?	Do you live near school?
C'est pratique.	It's convenient/handy.
Mon frère habite un grand appartement.	My brother lives in a big flat.
Son adresse est trente-six rue de la Gare.	His address is 36 rue de la Gare.
Ma sœur habite un village à la campagne.	My sister lives in a village in the country.
Nous habitons en centre-ville.	We live in the town centre.
Mon ami habite à côté de chez moi.	My friend lives next door to me.

C'est une maison à deux étages.	It's a two-storey house.
C'est une vieille maison.	It's an old house.
L'appartement est neuf.	The flat is new.
Derrière la maison, il y a un jardin.	Behind the house there is a garden.
Devant la villa, il y a un garage.	In front of the villa there is a garage.
Nous avons trois chambres.	We have three bedrooms.
Dans le salon, nous avons une télévision.	In the living-room, we have a television.
Les murs sont bleus.	The walls are blue.

Je range ma chambre.	I tidy my room.
Elle fait le ménage.	She does the housework.
J'aide ma mère.	I help my mother.
Tous les dimanches, je lave la voiture.	Every Sunday, I wash the car.
Ma sœur débarrasse la table.	My sister clears the table.
Je peux téléphoner en France?	Can I telephone France?
Le déjeuner est à quelle heure?	What time is lunch?
J'ai oublié ma brosse à dents.	I've forgotten my toothbrush.
J'ai besoin de dentifrice.	I need toothpaste.
Tu as du savon/une serviette?	Do you have any soap/a towel?
Je n'ai plus de shampooing.	I have no shampoo left.
La douche ne marche pas.	The shower doesn't work.
Où est ma chambre?	Where is my bedroom?
Elle est en face de la salle de bains.	It's opposite the bathroom.
Tu prends le petit déjeuner?	Are you having breakfast?
Tu veux mettre la table?	Will you set the table?
Où se trouvent les assiettes?	Where are the plates?

D'habitude, je me lève à sept heures.	Usually, I get up at seven o'clock.
Elle se couche à onze heures.	She goes to bed at eleven.
Tu as vu le film à la télé?	Did you see the film on TV?
J'ai regardé le match.	I watched the match.
Il écoute souvent la radio.	He often listens to the radio.
Qu'est-ce qu'il y a à la télé?	What's on TV?

LA MAISON

les pièces	rooms
la cuisine	kitchen
la salle à manger	dining room
la salle de séjour	sitting room
les WC	toilet
la cave	cellar
le rez-de-chaussée	ground floor
le premier étage	first floor

LE MENAGE

faire...	to do...
la cuisine	the cooking
les courses	the shopping
le jardinage	the gardening
le ménage	the housework
la vaisselle	the washing-up
le lit	(to make) the bed
laver	to wash
passer l'aspirateur	to vacuum
aider	to help

LES REPAS

le petit déjeuner	breakfast
le déjeuner	lunch
le goûter	tea
le dîner	dinner

Où habites-tu?
Tu habites une maison ou un appartement?
Où se trouve ta maison?
Parle-moi de ta maison.
Il y a combien de chambres?

Décris ta chambre.
Que fais-tu dans ta chambre?
Que fais-tu pour aider à la maison?
Tu regardes souvent la télévision?
Quelles sont tes émissions préférées?

LES MEUBLES

une armoire	wardrobe	un four	oven
un canapé	a settee	(à micro-ondes)	(microwave)
une chaise	chair	un frigo	fridge
un fauteuil	armchair	un lave-vaisselle	dishwasher
une lampe	lamp	une machine	washing machine
un lit	bed	à laver	
un miroir	mirror	une radio	radio
un placard	cupboard	une chaîne-stéréo	hi-fi
une table	table	un magnétoscope	video
un congélateur	freezer	un réveil	alarm clock
une cuisinière	cooker		

? CHECK YOURSELF QUESTIONS

Q1 Write in the missing word. (Look at pages 10–12 before you do this.)

A Mon frère _____ l'aspirateur.
B Tu _____ ta chambre?
C Nous _____ papa dans le jardin.
D Ma sœur _____ les fenêtres.
E J'_____ une télévision dans ma chambre.
F Tu _____ la vaisselle?
G Tu _____ besoin d'une serviette?
H Tu _____ le dîner à quelle heure?

Q2 Put the items (in the box) in the right room.

LA CHAMBRE
A _____
B _____

LA CUISINE
C _____
D _____
E _____

LA SALLE DE SEJOUR
F _____

le frigo
un fauteuil
un placard
la cuisinière
une armoire
un réveil

Answers are on page 149.

L'école est à deux cents mètres de chez moi.
Le centre-ville est à deux kilomètres.
J'ai une très belle chambre. Elle est verte et blanche.
Dans ma chambre, je fais mes devoirs et je regarde la télé.
Mes deux petites sœurs partagent une chambre.
Je partage ma chambre avec mon frère.
Tous les dimanches, je dois faire le repassage. J'ai horreur de ça!
Nous aidons tous à la maison – mes frères, ma sœur et mon père.
Mon frère n'aide jamais à la maison. Il dit que c'est le travail des filles.
Et mes parents sont d'accord!
Il me reste très peu de savon.
A la télé, je préfère les émissions sportives.
Je peux allumer la télé? Ça ne vous gêne pas?
Dans le journal, je lis des articles sur la politique.
Je trouve les films sous-titrés très ennuyeux.
Hier, j'ai vu une émission sur les lions. C'était passionnant.
Je regarde toujours le journal de vingt heures.
Chaque semaine, j'achète un magazine de mode.

School is two hundred metres from home.
The town centre is two kilometres away.
I have a lovely room. It is green and white.

In my (bed)room, I do my homework and I watch TV.
My two little sisters share a room.

I share my room with my brother.
Every Sunday I have to do the ironing. I hate it!
We all help with the housework – my brothers, my sister and my father.
My brother never helps in the house. He says it's girls' work.
And my parents agree!
I haven't got much soap left.
On TV I prefer sports programmes.
Can I put the TV on? Do you mind?
In the newspaper, I read articles about politics.
I find sub-titled films very boring.
Yesterday, I saw a programme on lions. It was fascinating.
I always watch the eight o'clock news.
Every week I buy a fashion magazine.

LES OPINIONS

C'est/C'était...	It is/It was...
affreux/affreuse	awful
drôle	funny
formidable	great
génial	wonderful

LES EMISSIONS DE TELE/DE RADIO

les informations	the news
un jeu télévisé	quiz show
un documentaire	documentary
une émission comique	a comedy programme
une émission musicale	a music programme
la météo	weather forecast
une publicité	an advert
un feuilleton	a soap/serial
un dessin animé	a cartoon
une pièce de théâtre	a play
en version française (en VF)	in French
en version originale (en VO)	in original soundtrack

When you are talking about your favourite programmes, try to use words like these, rather than English titles – *J'adore EastEnders* won't mean much to most French people, but *J'aime les feuilletons* will!

les informations

un dessin animé

une pièce de théâtre

la météo

? CHECK YOURSELF QUESTIONS

Q1 You are staying with a French family. How would you find out...

    A ...where the bathroom is?
    B ...how far away the town centre is?
    C ...if you can phone home?
    D ...if you can have a bath?
    E ...what time lunch is?

Q2 Put these sentences in the right order. Then add linking words and extra detail to make them into a full account.

    A Je me lave.
    B Je prends le petit déjeuner.
    C Je me lève à sept heures et demie.
    D Je vais à l'école.
    E Je m'habille.

Answers are on page 149.

How the grammar works

ER VERBS WITH MINOR IRREGULARITIES

acheter	to buy
j'achète	nous achetons
tu achètes	vous achetez
il/elle achète	ils/elles achètent

Some other verbs which gain an accent except after **nous** and **vous**:

geler	to freeze
mener	to lead
se lever	to get up
se promener	to go for a walk

....

espérer	to hope
j'espère	nous espérons
tu espères	vous espérez
il/elle espère	ils/elles espèrent

Some other verbs where the accent **é** changes to **è** except after **nous** and **vous**:

répéter	to repeat
s'inquiéter	to worry

....

jeter	to throw
je jette	nous jetons
tu jettes	vous jetez
il/elle jette	ils/elles jettent

Some other verbs where a consonant doubles except after **nous** and **vous**:

appeler	to call
s'appeler	to be called

....

envoyer	to send
j'envoie	nous envoyons
tu envoies	vous envoyez
il/elle envoie	ils/elles envoient

Some other verbs where the **y** changes to **i** except after **nous** and **vous**:

appuyer	to lean/press
balayer	to sweep
essayer	to try
essuyer	to wipe

One of the clear differences between a Grade C/D piece of writing and a Grade A piece is the accuracy of the verbs. The more verbs you can use correctly, the higher the mark you will get, not only for accuracy but also for Use of Language, where you get credit for the variety of your language. If you are limited to half a dozen verbs which you know well, your work is likely to be repetitive.

✎ Verbs – present tense

■ In English we can say:

1 I eat chocolate.
2 I am eating some chocolate.
3 I do eat chocolate sometimes.

The verb in each of these sentences in French would be the same:

1 *Je mange du chocolat.*
2 *Je mange du chocolat.*
3 *Je mange quelquefois du chocolat.*

■ The present tense in French works by a system of endings. There are three main types of verbs:

- *er* verbs, like *regarder* (to watch)
- *ir* verbs, like *finir* (to finish)
- *re* verbs, like *vendre* (to sell).

■ As well as making sure you use the right **personal pronoun** (*je, tu*, etc.), you need to get the **ending** right too. This is most important when you are writing, as it will affect your accuracy mark. In speaking, the question of endings doesn't make as much difference, since in the singular, whatever the ending, the sound will be the same for most verbs.

Look at these examples. Notice that the underlined words all **sound the same** for each verb:

ER VERBS

regarder	to watch
je <u>regarde</u>	I watch, I am watching, I do watch
tu* <u>regardes</u>	you watch, you are watching, you do watch
il/elle/on <u>regarde</u>	he/she/one watches, etc.
nous regardons	we watch, we are watching, we do watch
vous* regardez	you watch, you are watching, you do watch
ils/elles <u>regardent</u>	they watch, they are watching, they do watch

*For the difference between *tu* and *vous*, see Unit 6 (page 32).

NOTE:
- Verbs ending in *-ger* add *-e* in front of the *-ons* ending:
  nous mangeons

- Verbs ending in *-cer* add a cedilla under the *c* before the *-ons* ending:
  nous commençons

IR VERBS		RE VERBS	
finir	to finish	*vendre*	to sell
je finis	I finish, etc.	*je vends*	I sell, etc.
tu finis	you finish, etc.	*tu vends*	you sell, etc.
il/elle/on finit	he/she/one finishes, etc.	*il/elle/on vend*	he/she/one sells, etc.
nous finissons	we finish, etc.	*nous vendons*	we sell, etc.
vous finissez	you finish, etc.	*vous vendez*	you sell, etc.
ils/elles finissent	they finish, etc.	*ils/elles vendent*	they sell, etc.

✎ Reflexive verbs

■ We often use reflexive verbs when we talk about our **daily routine**. Most of these follow the pattern of *er* verbs, but they have an **extra pronoun**. Look at this example:

se laver	to have a wash
je me lave	I have a wash
tu te laves	you have a wash
il/elle/on se lave	he/she/one has a wash
nous nous lavons	we have a wash
vous vous lavez	you have a wash
ils/elles se lavent	they have a wash

■ The reflexive pronoun always changes with the subject pronoun:
   je me; tu te; il/elle/on se; nous nous; vous vous; ils/elles se.

■ The verb endings are the same as for ordinary *er* verbs.

Common reflexive verbs

se baigner	to bathe	*se raser*	to have a shave
se coucher	to go to bed	*se reposer*	to rest
se débrouiller	to cope/get by	*se réveiller*	to wake up
se dépêcher	to hurry	*se terminer*	to end
se déshabiller	to get undressed	*se tromper*	to make a mistake
se détendre	to relax		
se fâcher	to get angry	*se tromper (de)*	to get the wrong number (train, etc.)
s'habiller	to get dressed		
se moquer (de)	to make fun (of)	*se trouver*	to be (situated)

🥖 Common irregular verbs

- There are a lot of verbs in French which don't really follow any pattern, and which therefore **need to be learnt individually**. Here are a few you absolutely cannot do without.

avoir to have	*être* to be	*aller* to go
j'ai	je suis	je vais
tu as	tu es	tu vas
il/elle/on a	il/elle/on est	il/elle/on va
nous avons	nous sommes	nous allons
vous avez	vous êtes	vous allez
ils/elles ont	ils/elles sont	ils/elles vont

faire to make/do	*prendre* to take	*sortir* to go out
je fais	je prends	je sors
tu fais	tu prends	tu sors
il/elle/on fait	il/elle/on prend	il/elle/on sort
nous faisons	nous prenons	nous sortons
vous faites	vous prenez	vous sortez
ils/elles font	ils/elles prennent	ils/elles sortent

venir to come	*vouloir* to want
je viens	je veux
tu viens	tu veux
il/elle/on vient	il/elle/on veut
nous venons	nous voulons
vous venez	vous voulez
ils/elles viennent	ils/elles veulent

- Note that there are groups of verbs which follow a similar pattern:

Like *prendre*:

apprendre	to learn
comprendre	to understand

Like *sortir*:

partir	to leave

Like *venir*:

devenir	to become
revenir	to come back
se souvenir (de)	to remember

? CHECK YOURSELF QUESTIONS

Q1 How would you say this in French?

A I am listening to the radio.
B I have a wash in the bathroom.
C He is finishing his homework.
D Do you want to go out?
E I don't understand.

Answers are on page 149.

REVISION SESSION 1 ▬▬ What you need to know ▬▬

La santé

Ça va (mieux).
J'ai mal à la tête.
Ma sœur a mal au bras.
Tu as mal aux dents?
Je me suis cassé le nez.
Elle s'est cassé le doigt.
Je me suis fait mal à la jambe.
Il s'est fait mal au pied.
Ça fait mal, (là).
Elle est enrhumée.
Il a la grippe.
Hé! Attention!
Au secours! Aidez-moi!
Il faut aller chez le médecin.
Ma mère va à la pharmacie.
Je voudrais un rendez-vous avec le dentiste.
Je suis allergique à l'aspirine.

Health

I'm fine (better).
I have a headache (a pain in my head).
My sister's arm hurts.
Do you have toothache?
I've broken my nose.
She's broken her finger.
I've hurt my leg.
He's hurt his foot.
It hurts, (there).
She has a cold.
He has flu.
Hey! Watch out!
Help! Help me!
You must go to the doctor's.
My mother's going to the chemist's.
I'd like an appointment with the dentist.
I'm allergic to aspirin.

AVOIR

avoir besoin (de)	to need
avoir chaud	to be warm/hot
avoir faim	to be hungry
avoir de la fièvre	to have a temperature
avoir froid	to be cold
avoir mal (à)	to have a pain (in)
avoir raison	to be right
avoir soif	to be thirsty
avoir sommeil	to be sleepy
avoir tort	to be wrong

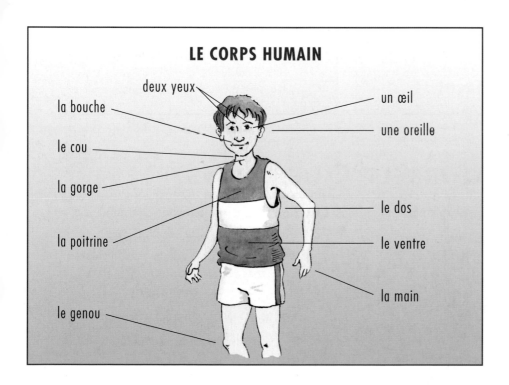

LE CORPS HUMAIN

deux yeux
la bouche
le cou
la gorge
la poitrine
le genou
un œil
une oreille
le dos
le ventre
la main

A TABLE

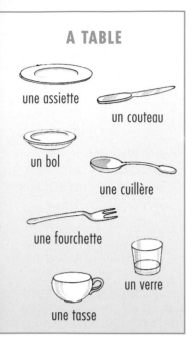

une assiette

un couteau

un bol

une cuillère

une fourchette

un verre

une tasse

La nourriture	Food
J'adore le poulet.	I love chicken.
Je n'aime pas tellement le chou.	I don't much like cabbage.
Tu me passes le sel/le poivre, s'il te plaît?	Will you pass the salt/pepper, please?
Je n'ai pas de fourchette.	I haven't got a fork.
Monsieur/Mademoiselle/Madame, s'il vous plaît.	(to attract the waiter's attention)
Je voudrais une table pour quatre personnes.	I'd like a table for four.
Je voudrais le menu à 12 euros.	I'd like the 12 euro menu.
Vous pouvez me donner la carte, s'il vous plaît?	Can you give me the menu, please?
Le service est compris?	Is the service charge included?
Où sont les toilettes/les téléphones?	Where are the toilets/the telephones?
L'addition, s'il vous plaît.	Can I have the bill, please?
Pour commencer, je prends du jambon.	To start, I'll have some ham.
Comme plat principal, je voudrais la truite.	For my main course, I'll have trout.
Qu'est-ce que vous avez comme dessert?	What sort of puddings do you have?

A LA CARTE

un croque-monsieur	a toasted ham and cheese sandwich
les crudités	salad of raw vegetables
les fruits de mer	seafood
un hors-d'œuvre	starter
le plat du jour	today's special
le potage du jour	soup of the day

QUESTIONS/PROMPTS

Qu'est-ce que vous aimez manger?
Il y a quelque chose que vous n'aimez pas?
Quel est votre plat préféré?
Que faites-vous pour garder la forme?
Est-ce que vous mangez sain?
Vous aimez la cuisine française?
Vous allez souvent au restaurant?

? CHECK YOURSELF QUESTIONS

Q1 Tell the doctor what the problem is.

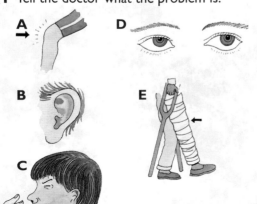

A

B

C

D

E

Q2 How would you tell your penfriend…

A … that you haven't got a knife?
B … that you don't really like chicken?
C … that you are not hungry?
D … that you need an aspirin?

And how would you ask him/her…

E … to pass you a spoon?

Answers are on page 150.

Higher vocabulary

Je me suis fait mal au genou en jouant au tennis.	I hurt my knee while playing tennis.
Prenez ces comprimés trois fois par jour, après les repas.	Take these tablets three times a day after meals.
Je vais vous donner une ordonnance. Prenez deux cuillerées du sirop avant de vous coucher.	I'll give you a prescription. Take two spoonfuls of the linctus before you go to bed.
Qu'est-ce que c'est exactement, la bouillabaisse?	What is bouillabaisse exactly?
C'est une spécialité de la région.	It's a speciality of the area.
C'est une soupe de poisson.	It's a fish soup.
Tu en veux encore?	Would you like some more?
Non, merci. Ça suffit.	No, thank you. I've had enough.
Oui, je veux bien. C'était vraiment délicieux.	Yes, I'd love some. It was really delicious.
On se met dehors, à la terrasse?	Shall we sit outside, on the terrace?
Mon steak n'est pas assez cuit.	My steak isn't cooked enough.
Pour la santé, il faut manger équilibré du pain, des céréales et pas trop de matières grasses, ni de choses sucrées.	For your health, you must eat a balanced diet – bread, cereals and not too much fat, or sweet things.
Il faut aussi mener une vie active.	You also have to lead an active life.

A LA PHARMACIE

le médicament	medicine
la crème (solaire)	(sun) cream
le sparadrap	sticking plaster

SE PLAINDRE

brûlé	burnt
froid	cold
immangeable	inedible
lent	slow
sale	dirty

COMMENT?

bien cuit	well done
à point	medium, just right
saignant	rare
nature	plain
à la française	French-style
grillé	grilled
vapeur	boiled

One of the skills which you are expected to have at Higher Level is the ability to cope with problems, and to handle the unexpected. This is particularly important in the role-plays, where you might have to return something you have bought, complain about something, or choose something else because your first choice is unavailable.

Make sure you know ways of:

- apologising: *Je regrette, .../Excusez-moi, .../Je suis désolé(e), ... mais ...*
- complaining: *Je voudrais voir le patron./Je voudrais me plaindre./Je ne suis pas satisfait(e).*
- saying what is wrong: *... ne marche pas./Il y a un trou./... est de la mauvaise couleur (taille).*
- negotiating: *Vous pouvez me faire une réduction?/Je voudrais un autre café.*
- choosing alternatives: *Alors, je prendrai une glace au citron./Bien, donnez-moi un sandwich au fromage.*

? CHECK YOURSELF QUESTIONS

Q1 In a restaurant, you have some complaints. What do you say when ...

- **A** ... your trout isn't cooked enough?
- **B** ... the service was very slow?
- **C** ... your coffee is cold?
- **D** ... there is a mistake on the bill?
- **E** ... the chips are burnt?

Q2 Complete the following sentences.

- **A** Je vais aller _____ cinéma ce soir.
- **B** Nous n'avons pas _____ carottes.
- **C** Vous avez _____ sandwichs?
- **D** Je voudrais _____ confiture.
- **E** Donnez-moi une glace _____ vanille.

Answers are on page 150.

How the grammar works

🥖 Nouns

- Most French nouns, like most English nouns, make their plural by adding –*s*:

une tasse	a cup
deux tasses	two cups

- There are **exceptions** to this rule:

  - Nouns ending in –*al* make their plural in –*aux*:

un journal	a newspaper
deux journaux	two newspapers

  - Nouns ending in –*eau* make their plural by adding –*x*:

un gâteau	a cake
deux gâteaux	two cakes

  - Nouns which end in –*s*, –*x* or –*z* stay the same in the plural:

un tas	a heap
des tas	heaps

- The most important thing to remember about French nouns is that they are always either **masculine** or **feminine**. Since the gender affects all the words that go with nouns (adjectives, pronouns, articles), you should always learn any new nouns together with a word (*un/une* or *le/la*) which tells you whether the noun is masculine or feminine:

le lait (masculine)	milk
la viande (feminine)	meat
un abricot (masculine)	apricot
une assiette (feminine)	plate

- Nouns referring to male people are masculine:

un neveu	a nephew

  Those referring to female people are feminine:

une nièce	a niece

- Otherwise, you simply have to learn the gender of nouns.

Indefinite articles

- *Un/une* ('a') and the plural *des* ('some') are used in the same way as their English equivalents, but you have to remember to use *un* before **masculine singular** nouns, and *une* before **feminine singular** nouns. Also, when 'some' is singular, you need to use:

  - *du* before masculine words:
    Vous voulez du sucre?   Do you want some sugar?

  - *de la* before feminine words:
    Je vais acheter de la confiture.   I'm going to buy some jam.

  - *de l'* before words which begin with a vowel:
    Je voudrais de l'eau minérale.   I'd like some mineral water.

- *Un/une* are, however, usually left out when talking about someone's job:
  Mon frère est chef de cuisine.

- All the above words are replaced by *de* after a negative:
  Je n'ai pas de chien/   I haven't a dog/any brothers/
  de frères/de café.   any coffee.

Definite articles

- In most cases where the English would use 'the', the French would use:

  - *le* before a masculine singular noun:
    le menu

  - *la* before a feminine singular noun:
    la table

  - *l'* before a singular noun (masculine or feminine) beginning with a vowel:
    l'oreille (f); *l'œil* (m)

  - *les* before a plural noun (masculine or feminine):
    les yeux (m); *les jambes* (f)

- However, the French also use the definite article to talk about something in general, while in English we leave it out:
  J'adore le chocolat.   I love chocolate.
  Je n'aime pas les animaux.   I don't like animals.

- When the words *à* ('to/at') and *de* ('of') come in front of the definite article, they combine in the following way:
  à + le = au   *de + le = du*
  à + les = aux   *de + les = des*

🥖 Present participle

- This form of the verb is used to show that one action happens **at the same time** as another:

Je me suis cassé le bras en faisant du ski.	I broke my arm while I was skiing.
En rentrant au bureau, j'ai trouvé beaucoup de messages.	On going back to the office, I found lots of messages.

- The present participle is formed by removing *-ons* from the present tense of the verb, and adding *-ant*.

  Regarder: (nous) regardons → *regardant*

  Faire: (nous) faisons → *faisant*

- As in the examples above, the present participle usually has *en* in front of it.

HIGHER
+
FOUNDATION UNDERSTANDING

? CHECK YOURSELF QUESTIONS

Q1 How would you say this in French?

A three horses
B some knives

C I don't have a spoon.
D I love ham.
E I eat chocolate while I watch television.

Answers are on page 150.

REVISION SESSION 1

What you need to know

Je m'appelle Claire.	My name is Claire.
J'ai seize ans.	I am 16.
Mon anniversaire est le 9 juin.	My birthday is the 9th June.
Je suis né(e) à Bruges.	I was born in Bruges.
Je suis belge.	I am Belgian.
Je suis fille unique.	I am an only daughter.
Je suis fils unique.	I am an only son.
J'ai un frère et une sœur.	I have a brother and a sister.

Mon frère est plus jeune que moi.	My brother is younger than me.
Il est marié.	He is married.
Sa femme s'appelle Ghislaine.	His wife's name is Ghislaine.
Ça s'écrit G-H-I-S-L-A-I-N-E.	It's spelled G-H-I-S-L-A-I-N-E.
Aujourd'hui c'est leur anniversaire de mariage.	Today it's their wedding anniversary.
Ma sœur est plus âgée que moi.	My sister is older than me.
Elle est divorcée.	She is divorced.
Elle a deux enfants, un garçon et une fille de six mois.	She has two children, a six-month-old boy and girl.
Ce sont des jumeaux.	They are twins.
Dans ma famille il y a cinq personnes.	In my family, there are five people.
Ma grand-mère habite chez nous.	My grandmother lives with us.

Je porte des lunettes.	I wear glasses.
Je suis grand(e).	I am tall.
Mon oncle est mince.	My uncle is thin.
Il a les cheveux longs.	He has long hair.
J'ai les yeux bleus.	I have blue eyes.
Ma tante est petite.	My aunt is small.
Mon grand-père est de taille moyenne.	My grandfather is medium/average height.
Il est très vieux.	He is very old.
Elle est assez vieille.	She is quite old.
Ma demi-sœur est sympa.	My half-sister is nice.
Mon demi-frère est agressif.	My half-brother is aggressive.
Ma belle-mère est aimable.	My step-mother is pleasant.
Ma sœur aînée est méchante.	My older sister is nasty.

Je m'entends bien avec ma famille.	I get on well with my family.
J'aime les sports.	I like sport.
Ma mère déteste la télévision.	My mother hates television.
Elle adore les animaux.	She loves animals.
Nous avons un chat, un chien et deux souris blanches.	We have a cat, a dog and two white mice.

LA FAMILLE

un bébé	baby
un cousin	cousin (male)
une cousine	cousin (female)
le mari	husband
la mère	mother
un neveu	nephew
une nièce	niece
les parents	parents
le père	father
le beau-père	step-father

LES CHEVEUX

courts   noirs

roux

frisés   bruns

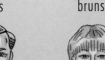

gris   blonds

LES YEUX

bleus	blue
verts	green
marron	brown

DESCRIPTION

beau (belle)	good-looking
gentil(le)	nice/kind
jeune	young
mignon(ne)	cute

LES ANIMAUX

un cheval	horse
un cobaye	guinea-pig
un lapin	rabbit
un oiseau	bird

QUESTIONS/PROMPTS

Comment t'appelles-tu?
Quel âge as-tu?
C'est quand, ton anniversaire?
Parle-moi de ta famille.
Il y a combien de personnes dans
   ta famille?
Quel âge a ton frère?
Tu t'entends bien avec ta mère?
Comment est ta sœur?
Tes parents sont séparés?
Tu habites avec ton père?

LES NATIONALITES

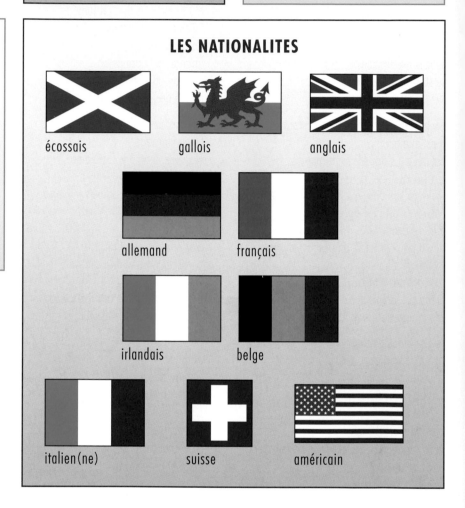

écossais   gallois   anglais

allemand   français

irlandais   belge

italien(ne)   suisse   américain

CHECK YOURSELF QUESTIONS

Q1 How would you say this in French?

   A My aunt lives with us.
   B He was born on 23rd September.
   C She wears glasses.
   D I get on well with my parents.
   E She has grey hair.

Q2 Correct the errors in the English.

   A Ma sœur a quinze ans.   My sister is five.
   B Elle n'est pas mariée.   She is married.
   C Il s'appelle Louis.   My name is Louis.
   D Mon grand-père a   My grandfather is 24.
       quatre-vingts ans.

Answers are on page 151.

Je ne m'entends pas avec mon père.
  Il est beaucoup trop strict.
Ma mère est adorable. Je peux lui parler
  de tout.
Mon petit frère m'énerve! On se dispute
  tout le temps.
Nous n'avons pas les mêmes goûts.
Je dois toujours rentrer à onze heures.
  Ce n'est pas juste!
Mon frère est vraiment gâté – il peut
  faire ce qu'il veut.
Il est plus facile de parler avec mes
  amis, si j'ai un problème.
Ils ont le même âge et ils s'intéressent
  aux mêmes choses que moi.
Ma petite sœur emprunte toujours
  mes affaires. Ça m'énerve!

I don't get on with my father. He's
  much too strict.
My mother is adorable. I can talk to
  her about anything.
My little brother gets on my nerves!
  We're always arguing.
We don't have the same tastes.
I always have to be home by 11.
  It's not fair!
My brother is really spoilt – he can
  do as he likes.
It's easier to talk to my friends, if I
  have a problem.
They are the same age as me and
  they are interested in the same things.
My little sister is always borrowing
  my things. It drives me mad!

EXTRA DETAILS

toujours	always
tout le temps	all the time
de temps	from time
en temps	to time
souvent	often
trop	too
vraiment	really
beaucoup	much/a lot
si	if
parce que	because

To do well at Higher Level, in both speaking and writing, you must express opinions. Make sure you have some ready-made phrases with which you can say how you feel about things:

> *C'est super* (great); *C'est cool* (super); *C'est génial* (brilliant); *C'est nul* (rotten); *J'en ai marre* (I'm fed up with it).

or about people:

> *Il est casse-pieds* (He gets on my nerves); *Elle est égoïste* (She's selfish).

? CHECK YOURSELF QUESTIONS

Q1 How would you say this is French?

  A We don't like the same music.
  B I can't come home after half past ten.
  C I get on quite well with my father, but I can't really talk to him.
  D My step-mother is older than my father.
  E Do you get on well with your brothers and sisters?
  F My best friend is called Marie. She is seventeen and she lives with her father. Her parents are divorced.

Q2 Do these people get on well (✓) or badly (✗) with their family?

  A Mes parents préfèrent toujours ma sœur – ce n'est pas juste!
  B Je suis fille unique, et mes parents me gâtent. Ils sont vraiment sympa.
  C Moi, je fais partie d'une famille nombreuse – quatre frères et trois sœurs – et c'est une famille très heureuse. Il n'y a jamais de disputes.
  D Ma mère, c'est aussi ma meilleure amie – mais on se dispute de temps en temps.
  E A la maison, c'est vraiment affreux. Heureusement que j'ai mes amis au collège.

Answers are on page 151.

Adjectives

- Adjectives usually come **after** the word they describe:
  Il a les yeux bleus.

- A few adjectives come **before** the word they describe:
  petit; grand; beau; gros; vieux; jeune

- When adjectives are used to describe a female person, or a feminine object, you usually add an *–e* to the adjective:
  ma petite sœur

  However, if the adjective already ends in *–e*, do not add another:
  Ma sœur est plus jeune que moi.

  BUT *Ma sœur est plus âgée que moi* (because of the accent *é*).

- When adjectives are used to describe more than one person or thing, you usually add an *–s* to the adjective:
  J'ai les cheveux courts.

  However, if the adjective already ends in *–s*, do not add another:
  Grand-père a les yeux gris.

- Note that nationalities do not have a capital letter in French.

- Some adjectives are irregular and do not follow the rules (see box left).

MASCULINE	FEMININE
agressif	agressive
italien	italienne
marron	marron
beau	belle
gentil	gentille
gros	grosse
mignon	mignonne
vieux	vieille
blanc	blanche

MASCULINE	PLURAL
beau	beaux
vieux	vieux
marron	marron

My / your / his / her

- Remember to say:
  mon *père* but **ma** *mère* or **mes** *parents*
  ton *frère* but **ta** *sœur* or **tes** *cousins*

- Remember that:
  son *oncle* can be **his** uncle or **her** uncle
  sa *belle-mère* can be **his** step-mother or **her** step-mother
  ses *amis* can be **his** friends or **her** friends

CHECK YOURSELF QUESTIONS

Q1 How would you say this in French?

A a small house
B My mother is taller than me.

C She is Italian.
D He has brown hair.
E My sister is nice.

Answers are on page 151.

What you need to know

Mon passe-temps préféré, c'est la lecture.	My favourite pastime is reading.
Le sport ne m'intéresse pas.	I'm not interested in sport.
Ça me passionne vraiment.	I'm a real fan.
Je collectionne les timbres.	I collect stamps.
J'adore le bricolage.	I love DIY.
Le théâtre m'intéresse beaucoup.	I'm very interested in the theatre.
Je passe tout mon temps libre à écouter des disques.	I spend all my free time listening to records.

J'adore les vacances d'hiver.	I love winter holidays.
L'année dernière, je suis allé(e) en Italie	Last year, I went to Italy
J'ai passé les vacances de Pâques à Londres.	I spent the Easter holidays in London.
On va à la montagne, ou au bord de la mer?	Shall we go to the mountains, or to the sea-side?
Je préfère aller à l'étranger.	I prefer to go abroad.

Hier, je suis allé(e) au complexe sportif.	Yesterday, I went to the sports centre.
Il y a une piscine, des courts de tennis et un terrain de foot.	There is a swimming pool, tennis courts and a football pitch.
Le soir, j'aime m'amuser.	In the evening, I like to have fun.
Si on allait à la foire?	How about going to the fair?
Au club de jeunes, on peut jouer au tennis de table.	At the youth club, you can play table tennis.
En été, il est ouvert jusqu'à dix heures du soir.	In summer, it's open till 10 o'clock in the evening.
Les billets coûtent combien?	How much do the tickets cost?
Ce n'est pas cher.	It's not expensive.
Ça coûte 2.30€.	It costs 2.30€.

Ce week-end, c'est la fête du village.	This weekend it's the village festival.
Il y a un 'son et lumière' au château.	There's a 'son et lumière' (sound and light show) at the castle.
Il y a un cirque sur la place.	There is a circus on the square.
Les zoos sont cruels.	Zoos are cruel.
Je ne suis pas d'accord avec toi.	I don't agree with you.
Mes parents me donnent de l'argent de poche.	My parents give me pocket money.
Je reçois quinze euros par semaine/par mois.	I get 15 euros a week/a month.

LES PASSE-TEMPS

les cartes	cards
les échecs	chess
les jeux-vidéo	video games
aller à une boum	to go to a party
aller en boîte	to go to a night club
danser	to dance
faire du camping	to go camping

LES FETES

le jour de Noël	Christmas Day
le jour de l'an	New Year's Day
la fête	person's 'name day' /saint's day (e.g. St David's Day for people called David)
la fête nationale (le quatorze juillet)	the (French) national holiday (14th July)

LES PRIX

enfants	children
adultes	adults
moins de treize ans	under 13
étudiants	students
réductions	reductions
dix pour cent	10 per cent
groupe	group

QUESTIONS/PROMPTS

Quel est ton passe-temps préféré?
Tu préfères le sport ou la musique?
Pourquoi?
Qu'est-ce qu'il y a à faire?
Où as-tu passé les vacances l'été dernier?
Tu reçois combien d'argent de poche?

le cyclisme

le foot(ball)

la natation

la planche

le rugby

les sports d'hiver

les sports nautiques

le ski (nautique)

le tennis

la voile

le volley

CHECK YOURSELF QUESTIONS

Q1 Read the following information, then put 'vrai' or 'faux' next to each sentence.

Au complexe sportif

- Prix normal d'entrée 3€ par personne.
- Offres spéciales ce week-end seulement.
- Trois entrées pour le prix de deux.
- Réduction de cinquante pour cent pour les groupes de dix.
- Etudiants — mois trente pour cent.
- Enfants de mois de quinze ans — 1€.

A Cette offre est valable tous les week-ends.
B Trois adultes paient 2€ par personne.
C Dix adultes paient 15€ en tout.
D Les étudiants paient 1€ par personne.
E Un enfant de seize ans paie 1€.

Q2 Match the two halves of the sentences.

A Ma passion, c'est les sports nautiques, …
B Je n'aime pas la lecture, …
C Je préfère les vacances d'été…
D J'adore faire du ski, alors…
E Je ne suis pas sportif, …

1 …car j'adore aller à la plage.
2 …j'aime mieux lire un roman.
3 …j'adore le ski nautique.
4 …je trouve les livres ennuyeux.
5 …je prends toujours mes vacances en hiver.

Answers are on page 152.

Hier, mon oncle nous a emmenés au parc d'attractions.	Yesterday, my uncle took us to the theme park.
Je n'aime pas tellement jouer au foot, mais je vais souvent aux matchs.	I don't much like playing football, but I often go to matches.
Moi, c'est le contraire. Je préfère participer que regarder – ça m'ennuie.	For me, it's the opposite. I'd rather play than watch – it bores me.
J'ai passé d'excellentes vacances en Suisse avec mes amis.	I spent an excellent holiday in Switzerland with my friends.
Moi, je suis allé(e) en vacances avec mes parents. Je ne me suis pas amusé(e) du tout.	I went on holiday with my parents. I didn't enjoy myself at all.
Mes copains/copines reçoivent plus d'argent que moi.	My friends get more money than I do.
Mes parents ne me donnent que huit euros par semaine. Ce n'est pas assez!	My parents only give me 8 euros a week. It's not enough!
Je dois acheter tous mes vêtements avec.	I have to buy all my clothes with it.
Il me faut travailler pour gagner mon argent de poche.	I have to work to earn my pocket money.
Si j'avais l'argent, j'irais aux Etats-Unis.	If I had the money, I'd go to the United States.

Create extra impact by stressing what you say. It makes it much more interesting.

- Change the impact of a negative by adding: *du tout* (at all); *tellement* (particularly); *souvent* (often).

- Point to a contrast by adding *par contre* (on the contrary) or simply *moi* (which stresses 'I').

- Use a variety of negatives: *ne ... jamais* (never); *ne ... que* (only).

? CHECK YOURSELF QUESTIONS

Q1 Choose the right word(s) to fit the blank.

A Il est tard, je dois _____ tout de suite.

B J'ai commencé _____ froid.

C Elle a essayé _____ à son frère.

D Tu as décidé _____ de bonne heure?

E Elle _____ à la gare à huit heures.

1	de téléphoner	6	à parler
2	te coucher	7	à avoir
3	est arrivée	8	est arrivé
4	partir	9	à me coucher
5	à être	10	de te lever

Q2 How would you say this in French?

A Last weekend, I went to Paris.

B My grandfather gave me eight euros.

C I have to do the housework to earn money.

D I like watching television.

E Yes, I agree with you.

Answers are on page 152.

▰ How the grammar works ▰

◁ The infinitive

- The infinitive of all French verbs ends in *-er*, *-ir* or *-re*. It is often translated as 'to ...' (for example *expédier* – to send).

- The most common use of the infinitive in a sentence is to enable you to use two verbs together. The **second** verb will be in the infinitive.

- Many common French verbs can be followed **immediately** by the infinitive:

AIMER	*J'aime jouer au football.*	I like playing football.
ALLER	*Il va regarder la télé.*	He's going to watch TV.
DEVOIR	*Je dois partir maintenant.*	I must go now.
SAVOIR	*Tu sais nager?*	Can you swim?
POUVOIR	*Je ne peux pas sortir.*	I can't go out.
VOULOIR	*Elle ne veut pas venir.*	She doesn't want to come.

- Some verbs need *à* before the infinitive:

COMMENCER	*Il a commencé à pleuvoir.*	It began to rain.
CONTINUER	*Je continue à travailler.*	I am continuing to work.
REUSSIR	*Nous avons réussi à ouvrir la boîte.*	We succeeded in opening the box.

- Some verbs need *de* before the infinitive:

DECIDER	*Nous décidons d'aller au cinéma.*	We're deciding to go to the cinema.
ESSAYER	*Il essaie de trouver un emploi.*	He's trying to find a job.
OUBLIER	*Elle a oublié de faire ses devoirs.*	She's forgotten to do her homework.

- Note also the following expressions which use the infinitive:

J'ai quelque chose à faire.	I have something to do.
Il est allé en ville pour acheter des vêtements.	He went to town to buy some clothes.
J'ai dit au revoir avant de partir.	I said goodbye before I left.

NOTE: If the verb is reflexive, think carefully about the reflexive pronoun:

Je me brosse les dents avant de me coucher.	I clean my teeth before I go to bed.
BUT *Elle se brosse les dents avant de se coucher.*	She cleans her teeth before she goes to bed.
Après avoir mangé, je suis sorti(e).	When I had eaten, I went out.

NOTE: For the verbs listed at the top of page 28, remember to replace *avoir* with *être*:

Après être descendu(e) du train, je suis allé(e) en ville.	When I had got off the train, I went into town.

✎ The perfect tense

- This is the tense which is used to refer to **events in the past.** It consists of two parts:

1 The present tense of *avoir*

j'ai	*nous avons*
tu as	*vous avez*
il/elle/on a	*ils/elles ont*

2 The past participle

This will end in –é for *er* verbs (e.g. *mangé*), or in –*i* for *ir* verbs (e.g. *fini*), or in –*u* for *re* verbs (e.g. *vendu*):

J'ai regardé la télé hier soir.	I watched TV last night.
Tu as fini ton petit déjeuner?	Have you finished your breakfast?
Elle a rendu le livre à Marie.	She gave the book back to Marie.
Nous avons attendu le car.	We waited for the bus.
Vous avez choisi?	Have you chosen?
Ils ont parlé avec le professeur.	They spoke to the teacher.

- The following verbs have irregular past participles, but otherwise follow the same pattern:

Infinitive	Past participle		
avoir	*eu*	*J'ai eu*	I had
boire	*bu*	*J'ai bu*	I drank
devoir	*dû*	*J'ai dû*	I had to
dire	*dit*	*J'ai dit*	I said
écrire	*écrit*	*J'ai écrit*	I wrote
être	*été*	*J'ai été*	I was
faire	*fait*	*J'ai fait*	I did
lire	*lu*	*J'ai lu*	I read
mettre	*mis*	*J'ai mis*	I put (on)
ouvrir	*ouvert*	*J'ai ouvert*	I opened
pouvoir	*pu*	*J'ai pu*	I could/was able to
prendre	*pris*	*J'ai pris*	I took
recevoir	*reçu*	*J'ai reçu*	I received
rire	*ri*	*J'ai ri*	I laughed
voir	*vu*	*J'ai vu*	I saw
vouloir	*voulu*	*J'ai voulu*	I wanted

- For a limited number of verbs, *avoir* is replaced by *être* when forming the perfect tense:

je suis	*nous sommes*
tu es	*vous êtes*
il/elle/on est	*ils/elles sont*

- The verbs requiring *être* in the perfect tense are:

ALLER	*Je suis allé(e)*	I went
ARRIVER	*Tu es arrivé(e)*	You arrived
DESCENDRE	*Il est descendu*	He went down
DEVENIR	*Elle est devenue*	She became
ENTRER	*Nous sommes entré(e)s*	We went in
MONTER	*Vous êtes monté(e)s*	You went up
MOURIR	*Ils sont morts*	They died
NAITRE	*Elles sont nées*	They were born
PARTIR	*Je suis parti(e)*	I left
RENTRER	*Tu es rentré(e)*	You went back/went home
RESTER	*Il est resté*	He stayed
RETOURNER	*Elle est retournée*	She returned
REVENIR	*Nous sommes revenu(e)s*	We came back
SORTIR	*Vous êtes sorti(e)s*	You went out
TOMBER	*Elles sont tombées*	They fell
VENIR	*Ils sont venus*	They came

For all these verbs, the past participle **agrees with the subject** of the verb.

- All reflexive verbs also use *être* to form the perfect tense:

SE LEVER	*Je me suis levé(e)*	I got up
SE LAVER	*Tu t'es lavé(e)*	You had a wash
SE RASER	*Il s'est rasé*	He had a shave
S'HABILLER	*Elle s'est habillée*	She got dressed
SE DESHABILLER	*Nous nous sommes déshabillé(e)s*	We got undressed
S'ARRETER	*Vous vous êtes arrêté(e)s*	You stopped
S'AMUSER	*Ils se sont amusés*	They had a good time
S'ASSEOIR	*Elles se sont assises*	They sat down

CHECK YOURSELF QUESTIONS

Q1 How would you say this in French?

A I'm going to listen to the radio.
B We did the washing up.
C He began to do his homework.
D They went to the cinema.
E She came back at ten o'clock.

Answers are on page 152.

UNIT 6: LES RAPPORTS PERSONNELS, LES ACTIVITES SOCIALES ET LES RENDEZ-VOUS

PERSONAL RELATIONSHIPS, SOCIAL ACTIVITIES AND MEETINGS

REVISION SESSION I — What you need to know

Enchanté(e).	Pleased to meet you.
Je vous présente M. Leblanc.	May I introduce M. Leblanc?
Voici ma sœur, Lucie.	This is my sister Lucie.
Entrez. Asseyez-vous.	Come in. Sit down.
Soyez le/la bienvenu(e).	Welcome!
Je vais te montrer ta chambre.	I'll show you your room.
Merci de votre hospitalité.	Thank you for your hospitality.
A demain.	See you tomorrow.

Ça te dit d'aller au concert?	Do you fancy going to the concert?
Si on allait au match?	How about going to the match?
Tu veux venir au cinéma avec moi?	Do you want to come to the cinema with me?
Je veux bien.	I'd love to.
Ce serait super.	That would be great.
Avec plaisir.	With pleasure.
Non, je regrette, je ne peux pas.	No, I'm sorry, I can't.
J'ai des devoirs à faire.	I have homework to do.
Je n'ai pas le temps.	I haven't got time.
Je dois me laver les cheveux.	I have to wash my hair.
On se rencontre à x heures.	Let's meet at x o'clock.
Si on se voyait devant la gare?	Shall we meet outside the station?
Rendez-vous au café.	Let's meet at the café.

Qu'est-ce qu'il y a au cinéma?	What's on at the cinema?
C'est un film d'aventures.	It's an adventure film.
C'est quel genre de concert?	What sort of concert is it?
Le concert commence/finit à quelle heure?	What time does the concert start/finish?
Je voudrais deux places, s'il vous plaît.	I'd like two seats, please.
C'était bien/intéressant/amusant?	Was it good/interesting/fun?
Non, moi, je l'ai trouvé ennuyeux.	No, I found it boring.
Mon acteur préféré est Gérard Depardieu.	My favourite actor is Gérard Depardieu.
Mon actrice préférée est Isabelle Adjani.	My favourite actress is Isabelle Adjani.

LES FILMS

un film d'amour

un dessin animé

un western

un film comique

un film policier

un film d'épouvante

LES SALUTATIONS

Bonjour.	Hello.
Bonsoir.	Good evening.
Bonne nuit.	Good night.
Bonne journée.	Have a nice day.
Bonne soirée.	Have a nice evening.
Bon appétit.	Enjoy your meal.
Au revoir.	Goodbye.
Salut.	Hi! / Cheerio.
A tout à l'heure.	See you soon.
A la semaine prochaine.	See you next week.

AU CINEMA / THEATRE

au balcon	in the balcony (upstairs)
à l'orchestre	in the stalls (downstairs)
la séance	the performance
le spectacle	the show
l'entracte	the interval
une place assise	a seated place
une place debout	a standing place

LES OPINIONS

moche	awful
chouette	brilliant
super	excellent

QUESTIONS / PROMPTS

C'est la première fois que tu viens en Angleterre?
Tu es déjà allé(e) en France?
Tu sors souvent avec tes amis?
Où vas-tu?
Qu'est-ce qu'il y a à faire à Paris?
Qu'est-ce que tu aimes comme films?

CHECK YOURSELF QUESTIONS

Q1 Your French friend has asked you to go out. How would you say the following in French?

A Say you don't like detective films.
B Say you have to do the housework.
C Suggest meeting outside the cinema.
D Suggest meeting at 7.30.
E Ask if he/she would like to go to the football match on Saturday.

Q2 Complete the following conversation.

A Tu veux sortir ce soir? (Accept the invitation.)
B On va au cinéma? (Find out what's on.)
C Un western. (Check what time it starts.)
D A vingt heures quinze. (Ask where you will meet.)
E On va au café après? (Say you have to be home before midnight.)

Answers are on page 153.

Higher vocabulary

On pourrait aller en boîte si tu préfères.	We could go to a night club if you prefer.
Tu veux m'accompagner au bal, ou peut-être au concert?	Do you want to go with me to the dance, or maybe to the concert?
Je regrette, mais vraiment je ne peux pas ce soir.	I'm sorry, but I really can't tonight.
Dis, demain c'est la boum de Joël. On y va?	Listen, tomorrow it's Joël's party. Shall we go?
Il y aura un monde fou.	There'll be a real crowd there.
Oh, je n'aime pas tellement les foules, tu sais.	Oh, I don't like crowds you know.
Tu es libre après-demain?	Are you free the day after tomorrow?
Non, disons plutôt huit heures.	No, let's say 8 o'clock instead.
La pièce était vraiment passionnante.	The play was really exciting.
C'est l'histoire de deux jeunes qui s'aiment, mais qui ne peuvent pas se marier à cause de leurs familles.	It's the story of two young people who love each other, but who can't get married because of their families.
C'est très triste.	It's very sad.

Many Higher Level tasks require you to offer alternatives, or to negotiate with other people to reach a satisfactory conclusion.

■ You don't have to simply accept or reject a suggestion; you can make alternative proposals of your own:

> *Tu veux venir au cirque avec moi?*
>
> *Non merci, je n'aime pas les cirques. On pourrait aller au concert si tu veux.*

OR

> *Je préférerais aller en disco.*

■ When you are making the invitation, you can offer alternatives:

> *Tu préfères aller au théâtre ou au cinéma?*

? CHECK YOURSELF QUESTIONS

Q1 Answer the following questions in French, using the appropriate pronoun(s).

A Tu veux voir un western? (You don't like them.)

B Il va chez le médecin? (He's going tomorrow.)

C Elle va écrire à sa mère? (She wrote to her yesterday.)

D Tu as des frères? (You have three.)

E Où sont les cerises? (Pierre has eaten them.)

Q2 Respond to these invitations, but check your diary first.

lundi après-midi:
chez Isabelle

mardi matin:
courses en ville

mercredi:
cinéma – 'Le Héros'

jeudi soir:

samedi:
pique-nique avec Marion

A Tu viens à la piscine lundi après-midi?

B Tu veux aller à la mer mardi?

C Mercredi, tu veux jouer au tennis?

D Il y a un bon film au cinéma cette semaine – c'est 'Le Héros'. On y va vendredi?

E Tu viens au match de football jeudi soir?

Answers are on page 153.

How the grammar works

✍ Subject pronouns

■ The most common pronouns are the subject pronouns which tell us **who** is doing the action of the verb:

je	I	*nous*	we
tu	you	*vous*	you
il	he/it (masculine)	*ils*	they (masc or masc + fem)
elle	she/it (feminine)	*elles*	they (feminine)
on	one/we		

■ The French do not distinguish between pronouns which refer to people and those which refer to things. What matters is whether the noun referred to is masculine or feminine.

Où est mon père?	Where is my father?
Il est dans le salon.	He is in the living room.
Où est mon sac?	Where is my bag?
Il est dans le salon.	It is in the living room.
Où est ma mère?	Where is my mother?
Elle est dans le salon.	She is in the living room.
Où est ma veste?	Where is my jacket?
Elle est dans le salon.	It is in the living room.

■ In the plural, *ils* is used to refer to a group of people/objects of which one or more are masculine:

Où sont mes frères et sœurs?	Where are my brothers and sisters?
Ils sont dans le salon.	They are in the living room.

■ There are two pronouns which are the equivalent of 'you' in English. The French use *tu* to a **person they know well**, to a relative or to a small child (or to an animal!), but *vous* to **strangers or adults** outside the family. So you would address your French penfriend or exchange partner and his/her friends as *tu*, but you would say *vous* to his/her parents and other adult relatives, as well as shop assistants, etc. Remember that *vous* is always used if you are speaking to more than one person.

✍ Object pronouns

HIGHER
+
FOUNDATION UNDERSTANDING

■ These are used to refer to the person/thing on the receiving end of the action of the verb. Like the subject pronouns above, they change according to whether the person/thing they refer to is masculine, feminine or plural.

■ The most common object pronouns are:

Referring to people		Referring to people or things	
me	me	*le*	him/it
te	you	*la*	her/it
nous	us	*l'*	(before vowel)
vous	you	*les*	them

- Unlike in English, these pronouns come before the verb:

Il m'a vu en ville.	He saw me in town.
Je t'ai envoyé une carte.	I sent you a card.
Elle nous invite à une boum.	She's inviting us to a party.
Où est ta montre? Je la cherche.	Where is your watch? I'm looking for it.

- When *la* (or *l'* referring to a feminine noun) is used in the perfect tense, the past participle should agree, by adding an *-e*:

Où est la limonade?	Where is the lemonade?
Je l'ai bue.	I've drunk it.

- When *les* is used in the perfect tense, the past participle should agree by adding *-s* (if it refers to a masculine noun) or *-es* (if it refers to a feminine noun):

Où sont les bonbons?	Where are the sweets?
Je les ai mangés.	I've eaten them.
Où sont les pommes?	Where are the apples?
Je les ai mangées.	I've eaten them.

- There is a special pronoun meaning 'to him' or 'to her'.

Ta mère sait que tu vas être en retard?	Does your mother know you are going to be late?
Je lui ai téléphoné.	I've phoned her.

  Lui becomes *leur* in the plural:
  Tes parents savent que tu vas être en retard? Je leur ai téléphoné.

Y/en

- The two pronouns *y* and *en*, which are not used in English, are never omitted in French.

- Reference to a **place** is made with *y*:

Qui va au cinéma?	Who's going to the cinema?
J'y vais ce soir.	I'm going (there) tonight.

- Reference to a **quantity** is made with *en*:

Tu as des crayons?	Do you have any pencils?
Oui, j'en ai deux.	Yes, I have two (of them).

Qui/que

- Both these pronouns can be translated into English as 'who' when referring to a person, or 'which'/'that' when referring to a thing. It can seem hard to know which to use, unless you remember the following rule:
  - Use *qui* when the verb comes immediately after:
    L'homme qui a volé l'argent. The man who stole the money.
  - Use *que* when the next word is a noun or a subject pronoun (see above):
    L'argent que l'homme a volé. The money (that) the man stole.

- Note that in English we often don't translate *que*, and simply leave it out.

Ce qui/ce que

■ When connected to one verb which comes before, and another which comes after, we use *ce qui* or *ce que* instead of *qui* and *que*. However, the above rule still operates:

Mangez ce que vous désirez.	Eat what you want.
Mangez ce qui est bon pour la santé.	Eat what is good for your health.

ORDER OF PRONOUNS

If you use more than one object pronoun with the same verb, they must go in the following order:

me   te   nous   vous

followed by

le   la   les

followed by

lui   leur

followed by

y

followed by

en

Demande de l'argent à ton père.
Ask your father for some money.

Il m'en a déjà donné.
He's already given me some.

Emphatic pronouns

■ These pronouns always refer to a person or people:

moi	me/I	*nous*	us/we
toi	you	*vous*	you
lui	him/he	*eux*	them/they (masc)
elle	her/she	*elles*	them/they (fem)

■ Most pronouns are linked with a verb, but emphatic pronouns are used in a number of different ways:

1 With a preposition:

avec elle	with her
chez vous	at your house

2 As a one-word answer:

Qui veut une glace?	Who wants an ice-cream?
Moi.	Me.

3 In a comparison:

Je suis plus âgé(e) que lui.	I'm older than him.

4 To emphasise a subject pronoun:

Moi, je préfère les films de science-fiction.	I prefer SF films.
Il n'est pas gentil, lui.	He's not very nice.

5 After *à*, to indicate to whom something belongs:

A qui est cet argent?	Whose is this money?
Il est à moi.	It's mine.

6 After a verb in the imperative:

Donne-moi ton cahier.	Give me your exercise-book.

CHECK YOURSELF QUESTIONS

Q1 How would you say this in French?

A I saw her yesterday.
B I wrote you a letter.

C the girl who is eating an ice-cream
D the boy I saw in town
E I'm going with you.

Answers are on page 153.

Unit 7: La Ville, Les Regions et Le Temps
Home town, local environment and weather

■ What you need to know ■

J'aime bien habiter à....
C'est une ville industrielle dans le nord de l'Angleterre.
J'habite à ... depuis cinq ans.
A ... il y a un musée.
Je préfère habiter en ville.
Il y a toujours quelque chose à faire.
C'est très bruyant.
C'est toujours animé.

I like living in....
It's an industrial town in the north of England.
I've lived in ... for five years.
In ... there is a museum.
I prefer living in town.
There's always something to do.
It's very noisy.
It's always lively.

J'aime mieux habiter à la campagne.
C'est un village typique.
On y est très tranquille.
Il n'y a rien à faire.
On devrait construire un complexe sportif.
Il manque une bibliothèque.
Il n'y a pas de distractions.
Demain, c'est la fête du village.
Il y aura un bal, une foire, un concours de boules.
On va en ville en car.
Le trajet dure quarante minutes.

I'd rather live in the country.
It's a typical village.
It's very peaceful there.
There's nothing to do.
They ought to build a sports centre.
It needs a library.
There aren't any entertainments.
Tomorrow, it's the village festival.
There will be a dance, a fair, a bowls competition.
We go into town by bus.
The trip takes 40 minutes.

Au printemps, on voit les petits agneaux.
En été, le soleil brille.
En automne, il fait mauvais temps.
En hiver, il fait très froid.
Quel temps fait-il en France?
En Angleterre il pleut toujours.
Il pleut/neige/gèle.
Il fait froid/mauvais/du soleil/du vent/ du brouillard.

Il ne fait pas très chaud aujourd'hui.
Voici la météo pour ce week-end.
Dans le nord-ouest, il y aura des averses.
Demain, il pleuvra.
Cet après-midi, il fera plus froid.

In the spring, you can see the little lambs.
In summer the sun shines.
In autumn, the weather is miserable.
In winter, it's very cold.
What's the weather like in France?
In England, it's always raining.
It's raining/snowing/freezing.
It's cold/miserable/sunny/windy/foggy.

It's not very warm today.
Here's the weather forecast for this weekend.
In the north-west, there will be showers.
Tomorrow, it will rain.
This afternoon, it will be colder.

A LA CAMPAGNE

un bois	a wood
un champ	a field
un château	a castle
une colline	a hill
une ferme	a farm
une forêt	a forest

EN VILLE

une boutique	a small shop
un hypermarché	a hypermarket
un magasin	a shop

LA METEO

dans l'ouest	in the west
dans l'est	in the east
dans le sud	in the south
il fera	it will be
beau	nice
chaud	warm/hot
il y aura	there will be
du soleil	sunshine
de la neige	snow
du vent	wind
du brouillard	fog
du verglas	black ice
des éclaircies	sunny periods
des nuages	clouds
Le ciel sera couvert.	The sky will be grey.
La température maximale/ minimale sera de dix degrés.	The maximum/ minimum temperature will be 10°.

QUESTIONS/PROMPTS

Vous habitez en ville ou à la campagne?
Vous allez souvent en centre-ville?
Parlez-moi de votre ville/village.
Qu'est-ce qu'il y a à faire?
Que faites-vous s'il fait beau?

A LA FERME

un canard

un cochon

une dinde

un mouton

un taureau

une vache

CHECK YOURSELF QUESTIONS

Q1 Look at the map and then complete the forecasts.

LA METEO POUR DEMAIN

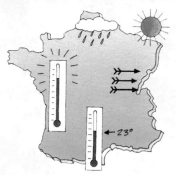

← 23°

A _____ il y aura du vent.
B Dans le nord _____ .
C Il fera très chaud _____ .
D Dans le sud _____ .
E Il y aura du soleil _____ .

Q2 Do the people speaking live in the town or the country?

A 'Il y a beaucoup de distractions.'
B 'En ville, il y a trop de bruit. Je préfère ne pas y aller.'
C 'Pour aller au cinéma, c'est un trajet d'une heure.'
D 'Le week-end, j'adore aller à la campagne.'
E 'Il n'y a pas grand-chose à faire.'

Answers are on page 154.

En France, il y a moins de grandes villes qu'en Grande-Bretagne.	In France, there are fewer large towns than in Great Britain.
La vie à la campagne est beaucoup plus agréable – en ville les gens sont toujours pressés.	Life in the country is much more pleasant – in town people are always in a hurry.
A ... il y a à peu près cinquante mille habitants.	In ... there are about 50,000 inhabitants.
La population de la France est pareille à celle de la Grande-Bretagne.	The population of France is the same as that of Great Britain.
La France est deux fois plus grande que la Grande-Bretagne.	France is twice as big as Great Britain.
Les paysages de France sont très variés: il y a des lacs, des montagnes et des plaines.	The scenery in France is very varied: there are lakes, mountains and plains.
A l'ouest, il y a la côte Atlantique, et au sud, il y a la Méditerranée.	To the west, there is the Atlantic coast, and to the south, there is the Mediterranean.
Le climat est plus doux qu'en Grande-Bretagne.	The climate is milder than in Great Britain.
En Corse, il fait très chaud, mais en montagne, il fait souvent moins cinq.	In Corsica, it is very hot, but in the mountains, it's often minus five.

One way of developing what you say is to use comparisons. This will make your sentences more varied and interesting, and also probably more accurate.

- Avoid stating absolutes (*Il fait chaud en France*) by making a comparison (*Il fait plus chaud qu'en Grande-Bretagne*).

- Adjectives of comparison can make your opinions clearer: *plus agréable, moins bruyant*.

? CHECK YOURSELF QUESTIONS

Q1 How would you say this in French?

  A Tomorrow, I will go to town.
  B We will have dinner at seven o'clock.
  C Will you watch TV tonight?
  D They will buy some CDs.
  E On Saturday she will be seventeen.

Q2 Write sentences in French, using these notes.

  Exemple: intéressant; télé; –; radio
       La télé est moins intéressante que la radio.

  A passionnant; voile; +; tennis
  B âgé; Paul; +; son frère
  C intelligent; les filles; =; les garçons
  D court; les cheveux d'Anne; +; les cheveux de Marie
  E amusant; les films d'amour; –; les westerns

Answers are on page 154.

▬ How the grammar works ▬

✑ Comparison

■ To use an adjective to compare one thing or person with another, put *plus* in front of the adjective and *que* after it:

> *Marie est plus âgée que Pierre.*   Marie is older than Pierre.
> *Les boîtes sont plus lourdes que*   The boxes are heavier than
>   *les paquets.*   the packets.

EXCEPTION: *bon*   good   *meilleur*   better

■ That is the most common form of comparison, but the following are also used:

> *Louise est aussi grande*   Louise is as tall as Claire.
>   *que Claire.*
> *Le car est moins rapide que*   The bus is less fast than the train.
>   *le train.*

Note that the adjective agrees with the noun as usual.

■ Adverbs can be used for comparison in the same way:

> *L'avion va plus vite que la*   The plane goes more quickly
>   *voiture.*   than the car.
> *Parlez plus lentement, s'il*   Speak more slowly, please.
>   *vous plaît.*

EXCEPTION: *bien*   well   *mieux*   better

✑ The future tense

■ The future tense in French is used in just the same circumstances in which we use the future tense (shall/will) in English.

■ Like the present tense, it works through a system of endings. The endings are the same for all verbs:

je	*-ai*	*nous*	*-ons*
tu	*-as*	*vous*	*-ez*
il/elle/on	*-a*	*ils/elles*	*-ont*

■ For *er* and *ir* verbs, these endings are simply added to the infinitive:

> *Je mangerai une banane.*   I will eat a banana.
> *Tu finiras les pommes de terre?*   Will you finish the potatoes?

■ For *re* verbs, the final *-e* is removed before adding the ending:

> *Elle attendra le prochain car.*   She will wait for the next bus.

**HIGHER
+
FOUNDATION
UNDERSTANDING**

■ The following verbs are irregular in the way they form the future, though the endings are the same:

ACHETER	j'achèterai	I will buy	FAIRE	je ferai	I will do
ALLER	j'irai	I will go	POUVOIR	je pourrai	I will be able
AVOIR	j'aurai	I will have	VENIR	je viendrai	I will come
DEVOIR	je devrai	I will have to	VOIR	je verrai	I will see
ENVOYER	j'enverrai	I will send	VOULOIR	je voudrai	I will want
ETRE	je serai	I will be			

The conditional tense

■ This tense is used to refer to what **would** happen (if something else happened). It is formed in the same way as the future tense, but the endings are as follows:

je	-ais	nous	-ions
tu	-ais	vous	-iez
il/elle/on	-ait	ils/elles	-aient

Tu voudrais habiter à la campagne?   Would you like to live in the country?

Il vendrait sa maison.   He would sell his house.

CHECK YOURSELF QUESTIONS

Q1 How would you say this in French?

  A Claire is not as tall as Marie.
  B She will make the bed.
  C They will come tomorrow.

D Will you be at home?
E I would prefer an apple.

Answers are on page 155.

REVISION SESSION I

What you need to know

AU ROYAUME-UNI

en Grande-Bretagne	to Great Britain
en Ecosse	to Scotland
en Irlande	to Ireland
au pays de Galles	to Wales

LES MAGASINS

l'épicerie	grocer's
la pâtisserie	cake shop
la pharmacie	chemist's
la librairie	bookshop
le magasin (de vêtements)	(clothes) shop
le bureau de tabac	tobacconist's (also sells stamps)

QUESTIONS/PROMPTS

Tu aimes faire des courses?
Quels sont tes magasins préférés?
Tu achètes beaucoup de vêtements?
Qu'est-ce que tu as acheté récemment?

Il y a une boîte aux lettres près d'ici?	Is there a post box nearby?
Où se trouve la banque la plus proche?	Where is the nearest bank?
Où est la poste?	Where is the post office?
Il y a une boulangerie à cinq cents mètres.	There is a baker's 500 metres away.
La boucherie est à côté de l'hôtel.	The butcher's is next to the hotel.
La charcuterie se trouve au coin, en face du supermarché.	The delicatessen is on the corner, opposite the supermarket.
Le magasin est ouvert de huit heures à vingt heures, sans interruption.	The shop is open non-stop from 8am to 8pm.
Nous sommes fermés le lundi.	We are closed on Mondays.
Je cherche un cadeau pour ma mère.	I'm looking for a present for my mother.
Quelle taille?	What size?
Quelle pointure?	What size? (shoes only)
Vous avez un pull vert, en trente-huit?	Do you have a green jumper, size 12?
Je peux l'essayer?	Can I try it on?
Je le prends.	I'll take it.
Il est trop long/court/cher.	It is too long/short/expensive.
Cette jupe ne me va pas.	This skirt doesn't suit me.
Vous l'avez dans d'autres couleurs?	Do you have it in other colours?
Non, je regrette, nous l'avons en gris seulement.	No, I'm sorry, we only have it in grey.
Vous pouvez me faire un paquet-cadeau?	Can you gift-wrap it for me?
Je ne m'intéresse pas à la mode.	I'm not interested in fashion.
Je voudrais un kilo de fraises.	I'd like a kilo of strawberries.
Et avec ça?	Would you like anything else?
C'est tout, merci.	That's all, thank you.
Je n'ai pas de pêches.	I haven't any peaches.
Je voudrais envoyer une lettre en Angleterre.	I'd like to send a letter to England.
C'est combien pour envoyer une carte postale?	How much is it to send a postcard?
Donnez-moi quatre timbres à zéro virgule quarante-six euros.	Give me four 0,46€ stamps.
Je voudrais changer un chèque de voyages.	I'd like to change a traveller's cheque.
La livre sterling est à combien?	How much is the pound sterling?
Allez à la caisse, s'il vous plaît.	Go to the cash desk, please.
Vous voulez signer ici?	Will you sign here?
On peut téléphoner d'ici?	Can you telephone from here?

LES VETEMENTS

des baskets

des bottes

une ceinture

un chapeau

des chaussures

un imperméable

un jean

un maillot de bain

un manteau

un pantalon

une veste

Femme

un chemisier

un collant

une jupe

une robe

Homme

des chaussettes

une cravate

une chemise

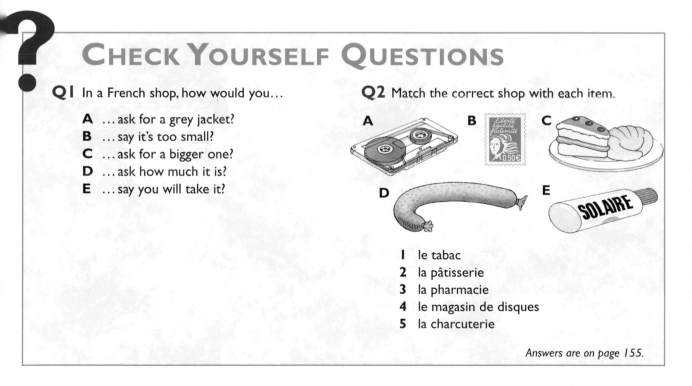

? CHECK YOURSELF QUESTIONS

Q1 In a French shop, how would you…

A …ask for a grey jacket?
B …say it's too small?
C …ask for a bigger one?
D …ask how much it is?
E …say you will take it?

Q2 Match the correct shop with each item.

A   B   C

D   E SOLAIRE

1 le tabac
2 la pâtisserie
3 la pharmacie
4 le magasin de disques
5 la charcuterie

Answers are on page 155.

LE GRAND MAGASIN

au deuxième étage	on the 2nd floor
au premier étage	on the 1st floor
au rez-de-chaussée	on the ground floor

LES REDUCTIONS

soldes	sale
moins 15%	15% off
offre spéciale	special offer
gratuit	free
bon marché	cheap
prix imbattable	unbeatable price

EN QUOI?

	(made of)
en argent	silver
en bois	wood
en coton	cotton
en laine	wool
en nylon	nylon
en plastique	plastic
en soie	silk
en verre	glass

Où est le rayon des disques?
L'alimentation est au sous-sol.
Vous trouverez les surgelés là-bas,
  à côté de la crémerie.
Tous les samedis, je vais en ville pour
  acheter des vêtements.
J'ai acheté ce baladeur ici la semaine dernière.
Malheureusement il ne marche pas.
Vous pouvez me le rembourser?
Mon ami m'a acheté ce T-shirt, mais
  il y a un trou. Je peux l'échanger?
La poche est déchirée.
Ce n'est pas la bonne couleur/taille.
Je voudrais envoyer ce colis aux
  Etats-Unis le plus rapidement possible.
Quand est-ce qu'il arrivera?
Ça coûte combien pour envoyer cette
  carte en Allemagne?
Je n'ai qu'un billet de cent euros.
Vous pouvez me donner des pièces de deux euros?
J'ai perdu mon sac à main hier.
Il est en cuir noir, avec mes initiales en or.

Dedans il y avait mes cartes de crédit,
  mes clés et de l'argent.
Je crois que je l'ai laissé dans le car.
On m'a volé ma montre Rolex il y a
  une heure à la gare.

Where is the record department?
The food department is in the basement.
You'll find frozen foods over there,
  next to the dairy produce.
Every Saturday, I go to town to buy clothes.

I bought this walkman here last week.
Unfortunately, it doesn't work.
Can you give me my money back?
My friend bought me this T-shirt,
  but there's a hole in it. Can I change it?
The pocket is torn.
It's not the right colour/size.
I'd like to send this parcel to the
  USA as quickly as possible.
When will it arrive?
How much will it cost to send this
  card to Germany?
I only have a hundred euro note.
Can you give me some two euro coins?
I lost my handbag yesterday.
It's made of black leather, with my initials
  in gold.
Inside, there were my credit cards,
  my keys and some money.
I think I left it on the coach.
My Rolex watch was stolen an hour
  ago at the railway station.

The more details you can give when you are describing something, the higher will be the level of what you say or write.

? CHECK YOURSELF QUESTIONS

Q1 What would you say when returning the following items to a shop?

A the radio you bought yesterday which doesn't work

B the blouse you bought on Saturday which is torn

C the jumper your mother bought you which is much too big

Q2 You are reporting the loss of your jacket. Give the following details.

A I left my jacket on the train.

B It's blue, made of cotton.

C In the pocket, there was a 20€ note…

D …and a gold watch.

Answers are on page 155.

◼ How the grammar works ◼

✎ Numbers

1	un	6	six	11	onze	16	seize
2	deux	7	sept	12	douze	17	dix-sept
3	trois	8	huit	13	treize	18	dix-huit
4	quatre	9	neuf	14	quatorze	19	dix-neuf
5	cinq	10	dix	15	quinze	20	vingt

21	vingt et un	70	soixante-dix
22	vingt-deux	71	soixante et onze
23	vingt-trois	72	soixante-douze
30	trente	80	quatre-vingts
34	trente-quatre	81	quatre-vingt-un
35	trente-cinq	82	quatre-vingt-deux
36	trente-six	90	quatre-vingt-dix
40	quarante	91	quatre-vingt onze
50	cinquante	92	quatre-vingt-douze
60	soixante		

100	cent
200	deux cents
201	deux cent un
999	neuf cent quatre-vingt-dix-neuf
1 000	mille (no word for 'a')
5 000	cinq mille
1998	mille neuf cent quatre-vingt-dix-huit
1 000 000	un million
1 000 000 000	un milliard (a billion)

◼ Percentages are written with a comma where we use a decimal point in English:

2,5% (deux virgule cinq pour cent) 2.5% (two point 5 per cent)

1st	*premier* (fem. *première*)
2nd	*deuxième* (sometimes *second* as in *seconde classe*)
3rd	*troisième*
4th	*quatrième* (the final *-e* of *quatre* is dropped)
5th	*cinquième* (notice the extra *u*)
6th	*sixième*
7th	*septième*
8th	*huitième*
9th	*neuvième* (notice the *f* becomes *v*)
10th	*dixième*

◼ Remember to use the simple number in dates (*le deux mars*; *le dix-huit février*). The 1st is an exception:

le premier mai   the 1st of May

- If you want to be less precise, you can use round numbers:

une dizaine	about 10	*une trentaine*	about 30
une vingtaine	about 20	*une centaine*	about 100

- Remember that in telephone numbers, the digits are paired. For example, 04 93 45 57 24 is said as follows:

  le zéro-quatre, quatre-vingt-treize, quarante-cinq, cinquante-sept, vingt-quatre

- All French telephone numbers now consist of ten digits, commencing 01, 02, 03, 04 or 05 depending on the area. If you need to say an English telephone number which has an odd number of digits, you should put together the first three digits, and pair the rest:

  01592 300158 → 015 92 30 01 58 (*zéro-quinze, quatre-vingt-douze, trente, zéro-un, cinquante-huit*).

☞ Quantity

- To refer to a specific quantity of something you can use:

  - a weight or liquid measurement:

un kilo	1kg	*un litre*	a litre
une livre	1lb/$\frac{1}{2}$kg (500g)	*un demi-litre*	$\frac{1}{2}$ litre
cent grammes	100g		

  - the container:

une boîte	a box or a tin	*un paquet*	a packet
une bouteille	a bottle	*un pot*	a jar
une cuillerée	a spoonful	*une tasse*	a cup
un flacon	a small bottle (perfume, etc.)	*un verre*	a glass

- Use the following to refer to quantities in a more general way:

assez	enough	*un peu*	a little
beaucoup	a lot	*tant*	so much
un morceau	a piece	*un tas*	a heap
(pas) trop	(not) too much		

- NOTE: All these quantities are followed by *de* before the name of the item, whether that item is masculine or feminine, singular or plural:

une cuillerée de sirop	a spoonful of syrup
un kilo de fraises	a kilo of strawberries
Ce soir j'ai un tas de devoirs.	I've got heaps of homework tonight.

- Fractions are also sometimes used to express quantity:

une demi-heure	half an hour
un demi-frère	a half-brother/stepbrother
un quart d'heure	a quarter of an hour

  But notice if the word 'half' is used alone:

Tu en veux combien?	How much do you want?
La moitié.	Half.

◎ Adverbs

- In English, we can turn many adjectives into adverbs by adding '-ly':

  happy → happily   quick → quickly

  In French, you can often do the same by adding *-ment* to the feminine form:

  lent (slow) → *lentement* (slowly)

  heureux (happy) → *heureusement* (usually in the sense of 'fortunately')

  malheureux (unhappy) → *malheureusement* (unfortunately)

- Adjectives ending in *-ent* or *-ant* become adverbs in a rather different way:

  évident (obvious) → *évidemment* (obviously)

  récent (recent) → *récemment* (recently)

  bruyant (noisy) → *bruyamment* (noisily)

- There are some common adverbs to which the above does not apply:

bien	well	*trop*	too much
mal	badly	*vite*	quickly
souvent	often		

- The adverb always comes **after** the verb:

  Je vais rarement au cinéma.   I rarely go to the cinema.

  Je le voyais souvent au centre sportif.   I often used to see him at the sports centre.

- Just like adjectives, adverbs can be used to make comparisons:

  Les Français parlent plus rapidement que les Anglais.   The French speak more quickly than the English.

CHECK YOURSELF QUESTIONS

Q1 How would you say this in French?

    A seventy-seven

    B ninety-five

    C twelfth

D 250 grams of peaches

E a glass of wine

Answers are on page 155.

REVISION SESSION I

What you need to know

LES PANNEAUX

Accès aux quais	To the platforms
Consigne	Left luggage
Douane	Customs
Passage souterrain	Subway

LES TRANSPORTS

un aéroglisseur	hovercraft
un car-ferry	car ferry
un taxi	taxi
un TGV (train à grande vitesse)	high-speed train
l'aéroport	airport
la gare routière	bus station
la gare SNCF	railway station
le port	port

LES INDICATIONS

à droite	right
à gauche	left
tout droit	straight on
la première à gauche	1st left
la deuxième à droite	2nd right
au carrefour	at the crossroads
au rond-point	at the roundabout

QUESTIONS/PROMPTS

Parlez-moi d'un voyage que vous avez fait.

Vous avez voyagé comment?

Quel est votre moyen de transport préféré? Pourquoi?

Comment venez-vous au collège?

Pardon, monsieur/madame.	Excuse me (to a man/woman).
Pour aller à la gare, s'il vous plaît?	How do I get to the station please?
Où est la station de métro?	Where is the underground station?
C'est loin?	Is it far?
Non, c'est à cinq minutes à pied.	No, it's five minutes walk.
Oui, il faut prendre le bus.	Yes, you have to get the bus.
C'est la ligne huit.	It's a number eight (bus).
Vous continuez tout droit.	You go straight on.
Aux feux, vous tournez à gauche.	At the lights, you turn left.
Prenez la première à droite.	Take the first on the right.
Je me suis égaré(e).	I'm lost.
Je cherche l'hôtel Ibis.	I'm looking for the Ibis hotel.
Je suis allé(e) en ville à pied.	I walked to town.

Je voudrais un aller-retour pour Paris.	I'd like a return ticket to Paris.
Donnez-moi un aller simple, deuxième classe.	Give me a single ticket, second class.
Je voudrais un carnet (de tickets).	I'd like a book of (ten) tickets.
A quelle heure part/arrive le train?	What time does the train leave/arrive?
Le train pour Lyon part du quai numéro sept.	The train to Lyon leaves from platform 7.
Je peux réserver une place?	Can I book a seat?
Le train est direct?	Is it a through train?
Non, il faut changer à Lille.	No, you have to change at Lille.
Le train 1234 à destination de Calais part du quai numéro trois.	Train No. 1234 to Calais is leaving from platform 3.
Le train 1157 en provenance de Marseille entre en gare, quai numéro cinq.	Train No. 1157 from Marseille is arriving at platform 5.
C'est bien le train pour Caen?	Is this the right train for Caen?
Cette place est libre?	Is this seat free?
Vos billets/passeports, s'il vous plaît.	Tickets/passports, please.

Le plein de super./Trente litres de sans-plomb./Vingt euros de gazole.	Fill it up with super./30 litres of lead-free./20€ worth of diesel.
Vous acceptez les cartes de crédit?	Do you accept credit cards?
Vous vendez des cartes routières?	Do you sell road maps?
Où sont les toilettes?	Where are the toilets?
Vous voulez vérifier l'eau/l'huile/la pression des pneus?	Will you check the water/oil/tyre pressure?

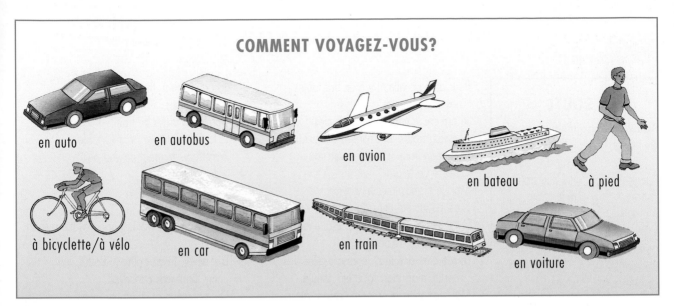

COMMENT VOYAGEZ-VOUS?

en auto

en autobus

en avion

en bateau

à pied

à bicyclette/à vélo

en car

en train

en voiture

? CHECK YOURSELF QUESTIONS

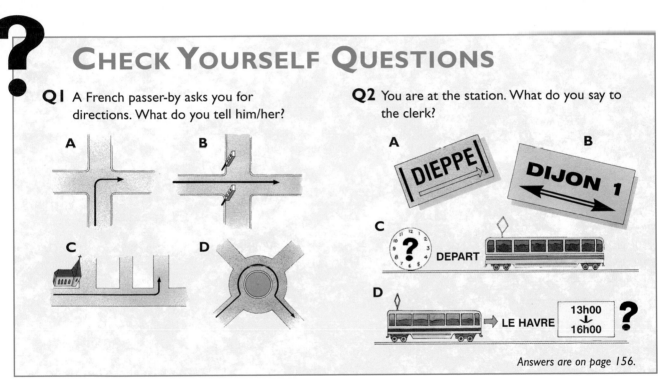

Q1 A French passer-by asks you for directions. What do you tell him/her?

A

B

C

D

Q2 You are at the station. What do you say to the clerk?

A DIEPPE

B DIJON 1

C ? DEPART

D LE HAVRE 13h00 → 16h00 ?

Answers are on page 156.

EN ROUTE

une autoroute (à péage)	motorway (for which you have to pay)
le péage	the pay-station
la sortie	exit
une route nationale (RN)	main road
une route de campagne	country road
le périphérique	ring road

EN PANNE

J'ai un problème avec:	I have a problem with:
la batterie	the battery
les freins	the brakes
le moteur	the engine
les phares	the lights
Je suis en panne d'essence.	I've run out of petrol.
J'ai un pneu crevé.	I've got a puncture.

LES PANNEAUX

Autres directions	All other routes
Déviation	Diversion
Toutes directions	All routes

Pour aller en ville, il y a un bus toutes les vingt minutes.

Je préfère voyager en train – c'est assez rapide, et c'est très confortable.

Hier, mon train est arrivé avec une heure de retard.

Moi, je prends toujours l'avion.

C'est beaucoup plus rapide.

D'accord, mais j'ai horreur d'attendre des heures à l'aéroport.

La semaine dernière, je devais aller à Berlin, mais mon vol a été annulé.

Moi, j'ai peur de prendre l'avion, alors je suis allé(e) en Belgique en bateau, malgré le mal de mer.

Si on prend la voiture, on part quand on veut – il n'y a pas d'horaires.

Mais ça coûte cher, et c'est polluant.

Et en plus, il y a des embouteillages.

Je suis tombé(e) en panne sur la RN13, entre X et Y.

Ma voiture est une Renault anglaise. Elle est blanche.

Le numéro d'immatriculation est KC51 YGC.

Vous pouvez m'aider?

Il y a eu un accident.

Un camion a heurté une moto.

Il n'y a pas de blessés.

To get to town, there is a bus every 20 minutes.

I prefer to travel by train – it's quite fast, and it's very comfortable.

Yesterday, my train arrived an hour late.

I always go by plane.

It's much faster.

Fine, but I hate waiting hours at the airport.

Last week, I was going to Berlin, but my flight was cancelled.

I'm frightened of flying, so I went to Belgium by boat, in spite of my sea-sickness.

If you go by car, you leave when you like – there are no timetables.

But it's expensive, and it causes pollution.

And what's more, there are traffic jams.

I've broken down on the RN13, between X and Y.

My car is an English Renault. It's white.

Its registration number is KC51 YGC.

Can you help me?

There's been an accident.

A lorry has hit a motor-bike.

No-one has been injured.

Q1 Last week, you went to Rome. Describe your journey.

A

B

C

D

E

Q2 Match the following statements with the appropriate means of transport below.

A Il y a toujours quelque chose à faire – un film, un repas – mais ce n'est pas très rapide.

B On arrive très vite, c'est vrai, mais je n'aime pas l'idée de voyager sous la mer.

C C'est mon transport idéal. C'est assez rapide et très confortable.

D C'est pratique, ce n'est pas cher, on est indépendant, et ça ne pollue pas. Mais c'est fatigant!

E Ça ne coûte pas très cher, mais c'est moins rapide que le train, et il y a quelquefois des embouteillages.

avion	car
voiture	bateau
train	vélo
tunnel sous la Manche	

Answers are on page 156.

How the grammar works

Asking questions

- There are three different ways of asking questions in French:

1 Putting the subject pronoun after the verb:

Tu as un chien.	You have a dog.
As-tu un chien?	Do you have a dog?
Vous aimez le chocolat.	You like chocolate.
Aimez-vous le chocolat?	Do you like chocolate?

NOTE: In this form of question, a hyphen links the pronoun and the verb. This form is most commonly used in writing, though it is also used quite often in conversation with question words:

Quel âge a-t-il?   How old is he?

NOTE: If the verb before *il/elle* ends in a vowel, an extra *'t'* must be put in.

2 Putting *est-ce que* in front of the verb:

Est-ce que tu parles bien le français?	Do you speak French well?
Est-ce qu'elle arrive en train?	Is she arriving by train?

This form is common in both writing and speech.

3 By ending the sentence on a rising tone:

Elle est anglaise?   Is she English?

This form can only be used in conversation.

- All these methods of forming questions can be used in any tense:

Est-ce qu'elles sont allées au cinéma?	Have they gone to the cinema?
Vous prendrez un café?	Will you have a coffee?

However, a little extra care needs to be taken in the perfect tense when inverting the pronoun and the verb:

Il a fini ses devoirs.	He has finished his homework.
A-t-il fini ses devoirs?	Has he finished his homework?

- Asking questions is an area where GCSE candidates tend not to do very well. In the exam, the role-plays will always expect you to ask at least some questions, and in many cases in the writing paper you will need to ask some questions as part of a letter.

If you are not very confident about your accent and intonation, it is probably better for you not to try the 'tone of voice' method. It is in fact possible to keep to just one method of asking questions. If you decide to do this, you should use *est-ce que*, although for the sake of a bit of variety, it might be a good idea to try to use the 'inversion' method in a few very familiar questions, for example:

Comment t'appelles-tu?
Où habites-tu?

✏ Question words

■ There are a number of question words which it is very important to know. You will need them in order to be able to ask questions, but they are also vital in order for you to understand the questions you will be asked in the conversation part of your exam.

■ The question words will often make the difference between understanding and not.

Où Where   *Quand* When   *Qui* Who

Où es-tu allé(e) en vacances l'année dernière?   Where did you go on holiday last year?

Quand es-tu allé(e) en vacances?   When did you go on holiday?

Qui est allé en vacances avec toi?   Who went on holiday with you?

Quel/Quelle/Quels/Quelles What/Which

Quel âge as-tu?   How old are you?

Quelle est la date aujourd'hui?   What's the date today?

Quelles sont tes matières préférées?   What are your favourite subjects?

A quelle heure arrive l'avion?   What time does the plane arrive?

De quel quai part le train?   Which platform does the train leave from?

Comment How (sometimes)   *Combien* How much/many

Comment viens-tu au collège?   How do you come to school?

BUT   *Comment est ta sœur?*   What is your sister like?

(To ask 'How is your sister?' you need to say: *Comment va ta sœur?*)

Tu reçois combien d'argent de poche?   How much pocket money do you get?

Tu as combien de frères?   How many brothers have you got?

■ *Pourquoi* Why

Pourquoi aimes-tu les maths?   Why do you like maths?

This is a very popular question in the conversation part of the exam, because it encourages you to give a detailed explanation, and it certainly almost forces you to answer in a sentence. The answer should usually contain *parce que*.

■ *Qu'est-ce que* What

Another very popular question, again because you can't just answer *Oui* or *Non*! You really ought to answer in a sentence if possible.

Qu'est ce que tu aimes manger?   What do you like to eat?

■ Finally, there is a very simple way in conversation of turning a question back to the person you are talking to:

Et toi?   How about you?

(It could be *Et vous?* if you were talking to an adult or a stranger.)

Tu aimes le sport?   Do you like sport?

Oui, j'adore le tennis et la natation. Et toi?   Yes, I love tennis and swimming. How about you?

CHECK YOURSELF QUESTIONS

Q1 How would you say this in French?

    A Did you like the film?

    B Do you often watch television?

    C What do you watch?

    D Where are you going?

    E What time do you eat?

Answers are on page 157.

UNIT 10: L'ENSEIGNEMENT SUPERIEUR, LA FORMATION ET L'EMPLOI
FURTHER EDUCATION, TRAINING AND JOBS

What you need to know

Je vais quitter l'école.	I'm going to leave school.
Je voudrais rester à l'école.	I'd like to stay at school.
Après le bac, j'espère aller à l'université.	After the bac (see Unit 1), I hope to go to university.
Si je réussis à mes examens, je vais aller en faculté.	If I pass my exams, I want to go to university.
J'ai étudié les langues.	I have studied languages.
Je veux étudier la géographie.	I want to study geography.
Je vais continuer mes études.	I'm going to continue my education.

Je voudrais être mécanicien.	I'd like to be a mechanic.
Je ne voudrais pas être facteur.	I wouldn't like to be a postman.
Il faut se lever trop tôt le matin.	You have to get up too early in the morning.
Ce n'est pas très bien payé.	It's not very well paid.
Je veux devenir professeur.	I want to become a teacher.
Je voudrais travailler en plein air.	I'd like to work outdoors.
Ma sœur est au chômage.	My sister is unemployed.
Elle cherche un emploi dans l'informatique.	She's looking for a job in computers.
C'est un métier intéressant.	It's an interesting job.
Mon père est électricien.	My father is an electrician.
Mon frère travaille dans une boutique.	My brother works in a small shop.
Ma mère est femme au foyer.	My mother is a housewife.

J'ai un petit job le soir/le week-end.	I have a little job in the evening/at weekends.
Je fais du baby-sitting.	I baby-sit.
Je travaille dans un restaurant.	I work in a restaurant.
Je livre le lait/les journaux.	I deliver milk/newspapers.
J'ai fait un stage dans un complexe sportif.	I did work experience in a sports centre.
J'aide les touristes.	I help tourists.
Je réponds au téléphone.	I answer the phone.
Je travaille le samedi, de huit heures à six heures.	I work on Saturday, from eight till six.
Je gagne quatre livres de l'heure.	I earn four pounds an hour.
Je fais des économies.	I put some money away.

LES LIEUX DE TRAVAIL

une bibliothèque	library
un bureau	office
un laboratoire	laboratory
un magasin	shop
une usine	factory

QUESTIONS/PROMPTS

Qu'est-ce que tu vas faire après les examens?

Tu espères continuer tes études?

Qu'est-ce que tu as l'intention d'étudier? Pourquoi?

Qu'est-ce que tu voudrais faire comme métier?

Tes parents, que font-ils dans la vie?

LES METIERS

un agent de police	policeman	un dentiste	dentist
un chauffeur (de taxi)	(taxi) driver	un ingénieur	engineer
un(e) coiffeur/se	hairdresser	un médecin	doctor
un garçon de café	waiter	un(e) serveur/se	waiter/ress
une hôtesse de l'air	air hostess	un(e) vendeur/se	shop assistant
un(e) informaticien(ne)	computer specialist	un vétérinaire	vet

une secrétaire

un fermier

une caissière

une infirmière

(Most of these jobs can be used to refer to a man or a woman, simply by changing *un* to *une*, or vice versa.)

? CHECK YOURSELF QUESTIONS

Q1 Tell your friend about your part-time job.

A

B 17:00 → 19:00   LUN MAR MER JEU VEN SAM DIM

C £25   LUN MAR MER JEU VEN SAM DIM

D

E

Q2 Que font ces personnes?

A J'écris des lettres sur l'ordinateur, et je réponds au téléphone.

B Les clients me donnent de l'argent, et je les aide à mettre leurs achats dans les sacs.

C Je me lève de bonne heure pour distribuer le courrier.

D Je travaille souvent avec les animaux.

E Je donne des renseignements aux touristes.

> … est facteur.
> … travaille au syndicat d'initiative.
> … est caissier.
> … est fermier.
> … travaille dans un bureau.

Answers are on page 157.

Je voudrais apprendre à taper à la machine.	I'd like to learn typing.
J'ai l'intention de devenir médecin, alors j'ai besoin d'aller à l'université.	I intend to become a doctor, so I need to go to university.
Pour être professeur de langues, il faut faire un stage à l'étranger.	To be a language teacher, you need to do work experience abroad.
Si on veut être informaticien, il faut être bon en maths.	If you want to work with computers, you have to be good at Maths.
J'ai décidé de quitter l'école.	I've decided to leave school.
Je voudrais travailler dans un restaurant – je veux être chef de cuisine.	I'd like to work in a restaurant – I want to be a chef.
Mon ambition, c'est de ne pas travailler. Je vais gagner à la loterie nationale.	My ambition is not to work. I'm going to win the national lottery.
J'ai choisi d'étudier les sciences et les maths – ce sont mes matières préférées.	I've chosen to study Science and Maths – they are my favourite subjects.
Je ne sais pas encore ce que je vais faire dans la vie. Ça dépend des résultats.	I don't know yet what sort of job I want to do. It depends on my results.
Je ne voudrais pas travailler dans un bureau.	I wouldn't like to work in an office.
J'ai horreur de rester enfermé(e) toute la journée.	I hate being shut up indoors all day.
Je préférerais travailler avec le grand public.	I'd rather work with the general public.
J'aimerais travailler avec les enfants handicapés.	I'd like to work with handicapped children.
Je voudrais être journaliste, mais il y a très peu d'emplois.	I'd like to be a journalist, but there are very few jobs.
Mon père est au chômage depuis deux ans.	My father has been unemployed for two years.

For this topic, you may well need to use past, present and future tenses – and probably the conditional too: what subjects you've done and what subjects you are going to do; a part-time job you've had, one that you do now, and the job you would like to do.

The topic also gives you many opportunities to give reasons for what you say, and if you've applied for a job, you will probably be asked about your experience, your qualifications (such as any foreign languages you speak) and your reasons for wanting this particular job.

QUELLE SORTE DE TRAVAIL?

dans un groupe	in a group
seul	alone
avec d'autres gens	with other people
avec les enfants	with children
avec les animaux	with animals

CHECK YOURSELF QUESTIONS

Q1 Choose a suitable job for these people.

A Je pense que la forme est très importante pour les adolescents.

B A l'école, je ne suis pas très forte, mais on me dit que je suis très sympa, surtout quand les gens sont malades.

C Au collège, je suis assez bon en sciences, mais ce que j'aime le mieux, c'est m'occuper de la vieille voiture de mon père.

D Je ne suis pas bon élève, mais j'aime voyager et rencontrer des gens.

E J'adore la mode et la beauté. Je ne veux pas travailler seule.

> informaticien
> médecin
> moniteur de ski
> coiffeuse
> chauffeur de camion
> mécanicien
> réceptionniste dans un cabinet de médecin
> professeur de gymnastique

Q2 Match up these halves of sentences.

A Je suis très fort en anglais et allemand, …

B Je vais travailler dans le magasin de mon oncle, …

C Avant d'aller à l'université…

D L'année dernière, j'étais faible en sciences, …

E Pourquoi est-ce qu'on travaillerait à l'école, …

1 … je vais passer une année en Belgique.

2 … quand il y a tant de chômage?

3 … alors je vais faire une licence de langues.

4 … donc je n'ai pas besoin d'aller en faculté.

5 … mais maintenant je vais travailler dur.

Answers are on page 158.

Negatives

ne ... pas	not
ne ... jamais	never
ne ... rien	nothing
ne ... personne	no-one/nobody
ne ... plus	no more/no longer
ne ... que	only
ne ... guère	hardly
ne ... ni ... ni	neither ... nor
ne ... aucun	not any
ne ... nulle part	nowhere

■ Remember to put *ne* between the personal pronoun and the verb, and *pas* after the verb:

Je n'aime pas le chou fleur.	I don't like cauliflower.
Il ne va jamais aux boums.	He never goes to parties.
Nous ne voulons rien.	We don't want anything. (We want nothing.)
Il n'y a personne dans la salle.	There is no-one in the room.
Tu n'aimes plus danser?	Don't you like dancing any more?
Elle n'a plus d'argent.	She has no more money.
Je n'ai que deux euros.	I only have two euros.
Il ne vient guère me voir.	He hardly comes to see me.
Elle n'a ni frères ni sœurs.	She has neither brothers nor sisters.

■ When the verb is in the perfect tense, the second part of the negative comes before the past participle:

Je n'ai rien mangé ce matin.	I didn't eat anything this morning.

An exception to this is:

Elle n'a vu personne.	She didn't see anyone.

■ *Personne*, and occasionally *rien*, can be used as the subject of the verb, but remember that you still need the *ne*:

Personne n'est venu me voir.	Nobody came to see me.

■ *Personne*, *jamais* and *rien* can be used as one-word answers:

Qui as-tu vu au club?	Who did you see at the club?
Personne!	No-one!
Jacques! Qu'est-ce que tu as dit?	Jacques! What did you say?
Rien!	Nothing!
Vous êtes allée à l'étranger, Marie?	Have you been abroad, Marie?
Jamais.	Never.

■ *Pas* can also sometimes be used without *ne*:

Pas ce soir.	Not tonight.

■ In conversation, the French often leave out the *ne*:
   C'est pas vrai!   It's not true!
   J'ai jamais vu un tel film.   I've never seen such a film.

You need to listen out for this in the Listening Test, though you should probably not do it yourself, and certainly not in writing.

The passive

HIGHER

■ This is a structure which is probably better not to try to use yourself, as it can lead to a lot of unnecessary errors. You may well come across it, however, especially in newspaper extracts:
   Trois voitures ont été détruites   Three cars were destroyed by a
       par un incendie sur   fire on the A6 motorway.
       l'autoroute A6.

■ The French often avoid it, especially in speech, by using *on*:
   On m'a volé mon sac dans   My bag was stolen in the metro.
       le métro.

CHECK YOURSELF QUESTIONS

Q1 How would you say this in French?

A We never go to the cinema.
B There is no more cake.
C She only has one brother.
D I didn't see anything.

Answers are on page 158.

Unit 11: La publicité, Les communications et les Langues au travail
Advertising, communication and languages at work

What you need to know

Quel est votre numéro de téléphone?	What's your telephone number?
Mon numéro de téléphone est le deux cent cinquante-trois, trente-neuf, quatre-vingt-quinze.	My telephone number is two five three, three nine, nine five (253 39 95).
Allô, M. Lenormand à l'appareil.	Hello, Mr Lenormand speaking.
Ici Jean-Luc.	Jean-Luc here.
Qui est à l'appareil?	Who's speaking?
Je peux parler au directeur?	May I speak to the manager?
Pourriez-vous me passer M. Martin?	Could you put me through to Mr Martin?
Je vous le/la passe.	I'm putting you through to him/her.
Ne quittez pas.	Hold the line.
Elle n'est pas là en ce moment.	She's not in at the moment.
Il est occupé.	He's busy.
Il peut vous rappeler?	Can he call you back?
Vous pouvez me contacter au...	You can contact me on...
Vous voulez laisser un message?	Do you want to leave a message?
Il y a un répondeur.	There is an answering machine.
Je rappellerai plus tard.	I'll call back later.

Il y a une cabine téléphonique près d'ici?	Is there a phone box nearby?
Il faut de la monnaie.	You need change.
Vous vendez des télécartes?	Do you sell phone cards?
Je voudrais téléphoner en Angleterre.	I'd like to phone England.
L'indicatif, c'est le zéro-zéro, quarante-quatre.	The code is 00 44.

Ce soir, sur la place du village, il y aura un grand bal.	This evening, in the village square, there will be a big dance.
Venez voir le cirque.	Come and see the circus.
Achetez vos billets à l'entrée, ou au syndicat d'initiative.	Buy your tickets at the entrance, or at the tourist office.
Je n'aime pas les publicités.	I don't like adverts.
Les pubs sont plus amusantes que les émissions.	The ads are more fun than the programmes.
J'ai vu l'annonce dans le journal.	I saw the notice in the newspaper.

DANS UNE CABINE TELEPHONIQUE

Décrochez le combiné.	Lift the receiver.
Attendez la tonalité.	Wait for the tone.
Introduisez les pièces.	Put in the coins.
Composez le numéro.	Dial the number.
Raccrochez le combiné.	Hang up.

French telephone numbers are now all ten digits long, and all begin 01, 02, 03, 04 or 05 depending on the area. The French put the numbers together in pairs, so 0153569620 is printed as 01 53 56 96 20 and said as: *le zéro un, cinquante-trois, cinquante-six, quatre-vingt-seize, vingt.*

LES FETES

le championnat	the championship
un concert	a concert
un concours	a bowls
de boules	competition
une foire	a fair
les gagnants	the winners
le gros lot	the big prize
les jours fériés	public holidays
un spectacle	a show
la musique	folk music
folklorique	

LES PETITES ANNONCES

cherche	wanted
à louer	for hire/to let
neuf/ve	new
d'occasion	second-hand
à vendre	for sale

QUESTIONS/PROMPTS

Vous aimez les publicités?
Quelle est votre publicité
préférée? Pourquoi?
Qu'est-ce que vous aimez
comme spectacle?
Vous avez déjà travaillé?
Où ça?

? CHECK YOURSELF QUESTIONS

Q1 What is being advertised here?

A Miami – au vrai jus de fruits.
B Dop – pour la santé de vos cheveux.
C La bonne musique moins chère.
D Chaque semaine, un poster géant.
E En vrai coton.

de la nourriture pour chiens
un yaourt
un magasin de disques
une machine à laver
un magazine pour les jeunes
un pull
des pommes
un shampooing

Q2 Fill in the missing words in these telephone messages.

A M. Dupont rappellera _____.
B _____ à Mme Leblanc ce matin.
C Mme Borie a _____ à six heures.
D Jeanne arrivera _____.
E Appelez M. Lucas au _____.

en retard	bureau
plus tard	arrivé
vous	téléphonez
rendez-vous	urgent

Answers are on page 158.

Vous pouvez m'envoyer un fax?	Can you send me a fax?
Marquez votre fax 'à l'attention de Mme Valadié'.	Mark your fax 'for the attention of Mrs Valadié'.
Vous pouvez me contacter par courrier électronique. Voici mon adresse.	You can contact me via e-mail. Here is my address.
Je dois écouter les messages sur le répondeur, et écrire des notes.	I have to listen to the messages on the answering machine, and write memos.
Je suis aussi responsable des photocopies.	I'm also in charge of photocopying.

Pour faire une demande d'emploi, il faut remplir un formulaire.	To apply for a job, you have to fill in an application form.
On m'a demandé de me présenter pour un entretien.	I've been asked to go for an interview.
Pourquoi est-ce que ce poste vous intéresse?	Why are you interested in this job?
Vous avez de l'expérience de ce genre de travail?	Do you have any experience of this sort of job?
Vous avez déjà travaillé dans l'hôtellerie/la restauration?	Have you any experience of hotel work/catering?
Parlez-moi de vos qualités personnelles.	Tell me about your personal qualities.
Je suis consciencieux/se, mais un peu timide.	I'm conscientious, but a bit shy.
Je m'entends très bien avec les autres/les enfants/les animaux.	I get on very well with other people/children/animals.
Quelles sont les heures de travail?	What are the working hours?
Quel est le salaire?	What is the salary?
Vous travaillerez du mardi au samedi, de seize heures à vingt-trois heures, et un dimanche sur deux.	You will work from Tuesday to Saturday, from 4pm to 11pm, and every other Sunday.
Le lundi, vous êtes libre.	You are free on Mondays.

Les publicités présentent toujours des idées stéréotypées.	Advertisements always show stereotyped ideas.
Le but de la publicité, c'est d'encourager les gens à dépenser plus d'argent, et à acheter des choses dont ils n'ont pas besoin.	The aim of advertising is to encourage people to spend more money, and to buy things they don't need.
Est-ce qu'on doit interdire certaines publicités?	Should certain advertisements be banned?

AU BUREAU

un(e) client(e)	customer
la direction	management
l'expédition	despatch
la photocopieuse	photocopier
le président	chairman
une réunion	a meeting

LA PUBLICITE

l'alcool	alcohol
les jouets	toys
la lessive	washing powder
la marque	brand
la nourriture	food
les produits	(household)
(de ménage)	products
le racisme	racism
la sécurité	safety
le sexisme	sexism
le tabac	tobacco
la vitesse	speed

LES QUALITES PERSONNELLES

aimable	pleasant, polite
de bonne humeur	cheerful
distrait(e)	absent-minded
élégant(e)	smart (in dress)
ouvert(e)	outgoing
ponctuel(le)	punctual
pratique	practical
sérieux	serious-minded
travailleur/se	hard-working

CHECK YOURSELF QUESTIONS

Q1 You are applying for a job in France.

  A Say you are free in July and August.
  B Say you have already worked in a restaurant.
  C Say you get on well with customers.
  D Say you would like to work evenings, but not weekends.
  E Find out how much you will be paid.

Q2 You are telling your friend about your new job.

  A You have to answer the telephone – it's difficult in French.
  B You have to help English customers.
  C You get on very well with the manager.
  D You have to work every other weekend, but you are free on Fridays and Mondays.
  E The salary isn't enormous, but it's not bad.

Answers are on page 159.

The superlative

- We have already seen in Unit 7 how adjectives can be used to compare things or people, by using *plus* (more), *aussi* (as) or *moins* (less).

    L'histoire est plus intéressante   History is more interesting
    que la géographie.   than Geography.

- A similar structure is used to identify someone or something as the most (or the least). Simply put the definite article before *plus* (or *moins*). This is known as the superlative form.

    La matière la plus intéressante,   The most interesting subject
    c'est la biologie.   is Biology.

- Note that the adjective (and the article) agree with the noun:

    Jean est le garçon le plus   John is the most hard-working boy.
    travailleur

    Ce sont les élèves les plus   They are the most intelligent pupils.
    intelligents.

- The adjective keeps its usual position. In the case of most adjectives, the adjective follows the noun. However, if it is an adjective which comes before the noun (see Unit 4), the superlative also comes before:

    C'est la plus petite entreprise.   It's the smallest firm.
    On a vu les plus beaux animaux.   We saw the most beautiful animals.

- While the superlative in English is often followed by 'in', in French it is followed by *de*:

    C'est l'élève le moins intelligent   He's the least intelligent pupil **in**
    de la classe.   the class.

    C'est la montagne la plus haute   It's the highest mountain **in**
    du monde.   **the** world.

    The following superlatives are the exceptions:
    bon → meilleur (better) *→ le meilleur* (the best)
    mauvais → pire (worse) *→ le pire* (the worst)

- The superlative of adverbs is formed in the same way as the superlative of adjectives:

    C'est Hélène qui court le plus vite.   It's Hélène who runs most quickly.

    Note that, since adverbs do not agree, there are no feminine or plural forms.

✑ Demonstrative adjectives

■ In French, the same words are usually used for both 'this' and 'that':

ce message (masculine)	this/that message
cette lettre (feminine)	this/that letter
ces publicités (plural)	these/those advertisements

■ There is another form – *cet* – which is used only before a masculine singular noun beginning with a vowel or with the letter *h*:

cet emploi	this/that job
cet homme	this/that man

✑ Demonstrative pronouns

celui (masculine)	*celle* (feminine)
ceux (masculine plural)	*celles* (feminine plural)

■ Like demonstrative adjectives, these are usually used to distinguish between two similar objects or people:

Je trouve que Nathalie est vraiment adorable. Tu sais, celle aux cheveux blonds.	I think Nathalie is really lovely. You know, the one with the blond hair.
J'ai vu ce film. Tu sais, celui avec Gérard Depardieu.	I've seen that film. You know, the one with Gérard Depardieu.
Tu n'aimes pas les documentaires? Même pas ceux avec les animaux?	Don't you like documentaries? Not even the ones with animals?
J'adore les pâtisseries, surtout celles avec de la crème.	I love pastries, especially the ones with cream.

■ When no specific thing is referred to, use *ceci* or *cela* (often shortened to *ça*).

Marc m'a donné ceci.	Marc gave me this.
Je n'ai jamais vu ça.	I've never seen that.

? CHECK YOURSELF QUESTIONS

Q1 How would you say this in French?

A He is the most intelligent boy in the school.

B It's the most amusing advert.

C I don't like that teacher.

D I love that programme.

Answers are on page 159.

UNIT 12: LA VIE A L'ETRANGER, LE TOURISME, LES COUTUMES ET LE LOGEMENT
CUSTOMS AND ACCOMMODATION

What you need to know

Pendant les grandes vacances, j'ai passé une semaine sur la côte d'Azur.	During the summer holidays, I spent a week on the Mediterranean coast.
Je me suis très bien amusé(e).	I had a very good time.
C'était une jolie région.	It was a pretty area.
Il a fait beau.	The weather was good.
L'hôtel était excellent.	The hotel was excellent.
Nous avons très bien mangé.	We ate very well.
Nous sommes allés dans beaucoup de musées.	We went to a lot of museums.
C'était ennuyeux.	It was boring.

Vous avez une chambre pour deux personnes pour ce soir?	Do you have a double room for tonight?
avec douche/salle de bains/WC?	with shower/bathroom/toilet?
avec un grand lit/deux lits?	with a double bed/two single beds?
C'est pour deux nuits.	It's for two nights.
Je voudrais réserver une chambre.	I'd like to book a room.
La chambre est vingt-trois euros la nuit.	The room is 23€ per night.
Le petit déjeuner coûte six euros par personne.	Breakfast costs 6€ per person.
Le petit déjeuner est de sept heures à huit heures trente.	Breakfast is from 7 to 8.30.
Je peux voir la chambre?	Can I see the room?
Il n'y a pas d'oreillers/de couvertures/de serviettes.	There are no pillows/blankets/towels.
Il y a une salle de bains à chaque étage.	There is a bathroom on each floor.

Le garage est derrière l'hôtel.	The garage is behind the hotel.
Il y a une auberge de jeunesse près de la gare.	There is a youth hostel near the station.
Il est interdit de faire la cuisine dans les dortoirs.	Cooking in the dormitories is forbidden.
Je regrette, le camping est complet.	I'm sorry, the campsite is full.
Votre emplacement est tout près des bacs à vaisselle.	Your pitch is right next to the washing-up sinks.
Vous pouvez louer des draps/des sacs de couchage.	You can hire sheets/sleeping bags.

AU CAMPING

par personne	per person
par tente	per tent
par nuit	per night
par emplacement	per pitch
par caravane	per caravan
les sanitaires	the shower/ lavatory blocks
les poubelles	the dustbins
l'aire de jeux	the play area

LE REGLEMENT DE L'AUBERGE

Il est interdit de:	You must not:
faire du bruit	make a noise
préparer les repas	prepare meals
faire la lessive	do your washing

Il faut:	You must:
rentrer avant onze heures	be back before 11
nettoyer la cuisine	clean the kitchen

QUESTIONS/PROMPTS

Tu as déjà fait du camping?
Tu préfères passer les vacances à l'hôtel ou au camping? Pourquoi?
Tu aimes la cuisine étrangère? Laquelle?
Où passes-tu tes vacances d'habitude?
Parle-moi de tes vacances l'année dernière.

Q1 You are at a hotel. What do you say?

A

B

C

D

E

Q2 Fill in the gaps in the following sentences.

A Vous avez un _____ pour une tente et une caravane?

B Vous êtes priés de ne pas faire de bruit _____ dix heures du soir.

C L'auberge est _____ entre dix heures et demie et sept heures.

D Vous êtes priés de faire la vaisselle _____ de partir.

E Le _____ des filles est au premier étage, à droite.

fermée	emplacement
restaurant	dortoir
garage	avant
ouverte	vers
après	

Answers are on page 160.

La bouillabaisse est une sorte de soupe de poisson.	Bouillabaisse is a sort of fish soup.
Pour faire une crème caramel pour quatre personnes, il vous faut un litre de lait, 250 grammes de sucre, et six œufs.	To make a creme caramel for four people, you need a litre of milk, 250 grams of sugar and six eggs.
En France, on mange généralement assez tard le soir.	In France, they usually eat quite late in the evening.
Dis, on se tutoie maintenant?	Shall we call each other 'tu' now?

J'ai l'intention de visiter votre région au mois de juillet prochain.	I intend to visit your area next July.
Pourriez-vous m'envoyer un plan de la région et une liste des hôtels?	Could you send me a map of the region and a list of hotels?
Avez-vous des brochures sur les excursions et les sites touristiques?	Do you have any brochures about excursions and tourist attractions?
L'année prochaine, j'irai au Kenya faire un safari. Ce sera passionnant de voir tous les animaux sauvages.	Next year, I'm going on a safari in Kenya. It will be exciting to see all the wild animals.
Je préfère les vacances actives – cette année, par exemple, je vais faire du canoë-kayak.	I prefer active holidays – this year, for example, I'm going canoeing.
Moi, par contre, je vais en vacances pour me détendre: quinze jours sur une plage avec un bon livre, voilà l'idéal.	For me, it's the opposite. I go on holiday to relax: a fortnight on a beach with a good book, that's my ideal.
Ah non! Ça m'ennuierait énormément.	Oh no. I'd be terribly bored.

Vraiment, ça ne va pas. Il n'y a pas d'eau chaude, et la chambre est sale.	Really, this won't do. There's no hot water, and the room is dirty.
Je n'arrive pas à dormir. Il y a du bruit au bar jusqu'à deux heures du matin.	I can't get to sleep. There's noise in the bar until two in the morning.
Il y a un robinet qui goutte. Vous pouvez envoyer quelqu'un?	There's a dripping tap. Can you send someone?
Il y a de la circulation toute la nuit.	There's traffic all night.
Vous pouvez me trouver une autre chambre?	Can you find me another room?

LES RECETTES

ajoutez	add
battez	beat
faites bouillir	boil
faites chauffer	heat
faites frire	fry
au four	in the oven
dans une poêle	in a frying-pan
mélangez	mix
versez	pour

L'HOTEL

les arrhes	deposit
un ascenseur	a lift
confirmer (par écrit)	to confirm (in writing)
pension complète	full board (room with breakfast, lunch and evening meal)
demi-pension	half board (room with breakfast and evening meal)
une réservation	a reservation
une salle de jeux	a games room

LES EXCURSIONS

la cathédrale	the cathedral	le paysage	the scenery
une cité médiévale	a medieval walled town	la vieille ville	the old town
		une demi-journée	half a day
l'église	the church	une journée	a day
les îles	the islands	une soirée	an evening
un lac	a lake	à cheval	on horse-back
un monument historique	a historical monument		

? CHECK YOURSELF QUESTIONS

Q1 You are writing to a French hotel. What do you write?

A You want to book a room for two weeks...

B ...from the 23rd July to the 5th August.

C You want a room for two people, with shower and toilet, with breakfast and evening meal.

D You want them to send you some brochures about the region.

E You want them to confirm your booking.

Q2 Your friends are telling you about their holidays. Match each sentence with the appropriate person from the list.

A Ma chambre donnait sur la route nationale. Le bruit de la circulation était affreux.

B L'hôtel était impeccable, à cent mètres d'une belle plage. La cuisine était très bonne aussi, mais le soir ce n'était pas très animé.

C On était quatre, alors on s'est bien amusé. Mais les chambres étaient sales, et les lits n'étaient pas du tout confortables.

D Il a fait un temps splendide, on a passé toute la journée à la plage, et je me suis beaucoup ennuyée.

E C'était vraiment super. J'ai déjà réservé au même camping pour l'année prochaine.

Maryse, qui a passé de bonnes vacances malgré l'hôtel

Marc, qui s'est fait beaucoup d'amis

Samir, qui était content de l'hôtel, mais qui s'est un peu ennuyé

Rachelle, qui a passé d'excellentes vacances

Annie, qui est rentrée très fatiguée

Chloé, qui aurait préféré des vacances plus actives

Answers are on page 160.

 How the grammar works

The imperfect tense

- As with other tenses, the imperfect tense works with a system of endings. There is only one set of endings, which are used for all verbs:

je	-ais	nous	-ions
tu	-ais	vous	-iez
il/elle/on	-ait	ils/elles	-aient

- These endings are added to the *nous* form of the present tense, minus the *-ons*:

Nous regardons → regard → je regardais	I was watching
Nous choisissons → choisiss → je choisissais	I was choosing
Nous descendons → descend → je descendais	I was going down
Nous allons → all → j'allais	I was going

- The only exception to this is the verb *être*, though it uses the same endings:

j'étais	nous étions
tu étais	vous étiez
il/elle/on était	ils/elles étaient

- The imperfect tense is used for description in the past, and to describe repeated or interrupted actions in the past. In English, these are often expressed by 'was/were ...ing' or 'used to ...', but this is only a rough guide, and there are many exceptions. The only way to get to grips with the imperfect tense is by seeing it in action. Here are some examples:

Elle prenait le petit déjeuner quand le téléphone a sonné.	She was having breakfast when the phone rang. (interrupted action)
Quand nous étions jeunes nous passions toujours les vacances au bord de la mer.	When we were young (description) we always spent (repeated action) our holidays at the sea-side.
Je suis allé en France pour la première fois quand j'avais douze ans.	I went to France for the first time when I was twelve. (description)
Il fumait beaucoup, mais il a arrêté l'année dernière.	He used to smoke a lot (repeated action), but he stopped last year.

HIGHER + FOUNDATION UNDERSTANDING

The pluperfect tense

- This tense is used when the main action is in the past, and you need to refer to something which had happened even earlier. It is formed like the perfect tense, by using part of *avoir* or *être* and the past participle, but using the imperfect tense:

j'avais préparé	I had prepared
tu avais fini	you had finished
il/elle/on avait vu	he/she/one had seen
nous avions fait	we had done
vous aviez dit	you had said
ils/elles avaient eu	they had had

HIGHER + FOUNDATION UNDERSTANDING

j'étais entré(e)	I had gone in
tu étais parti(e)	you had left
il/on était allé	he/one had gone
elle était venue	she had come
nous étions retourné(e)s	we had returned
vous étiez arrivé(e)s	you had arrived
ils étaient sortis	they had gone out
elles étaient tombées	they had fallen

■ Reflexive verbs also use *être*:

je m'étais levé(e)	I had got up
nous nous étions couché(e)s	We had gone to bed

Remember the agreement of the past participle with verbs using *être*.

Venir de + infinitive

■ To express the idea of having just done something, use the verb *venir* in the present tense, followed by *de* then an infinitive:

Je *viens de parler à Marie.*	I have just spoken to Marie.
Ils *viennent d'arriver.*	They have just arrived.

■ This construction can also be used in the imperfect:

Je *venais de quitter* la maison.	I had just left the house.
Nous *venions de dîner.*	We had just had dinner.

Il y a

■ As well as meaning 'there is/are', *il y a* can also be used with expressions of time to mean 'ago':

Je l'ai vu *il y a dix minutes.*	I saw him 10 minutes ago.
Elle est partie *il y a une semaine.*	She left a week ago.

■ Note that *il y a* always comes before the time expression.

CHECK YOURSELF QUESTIONS

Q1 How would you say this in French?

A We were finishing our homework.

B She used to eat a lot.

C You had already gone out.

D The campsite was near the beach.

E I saw the film when I was in Paris.

Answers are on page 161.

REVISION SESSION 1

What you need to know

Tu as visité beaucoup de pays?	Have you been to many countries?
Non, je connais seulement l'Europe.	No, I only know Europe.
Nous faisons tous partie de l'Union Européenne.	We are all part of the European Union.
Je ne suis jamais allé(e) en Grèce.	I've never been to Greece.
Je voudrais aller en Inde un jour.	I'd like to go to India one day.
Quelle est la capitale de l'Italie?	What is the capital of Italy?
La capitale du Royaume-Uni est Londres.	The capital of the UK is London.
Au Québec (au Canada) on parle français.	In Quebec (in Canada) they speak French.
En Suisse, il y a quatre langues: le français, l'allemand, l'italien et le romanche.	In Switzerland, there are four languages: French, German, Italian and Romansh.

C'est un tennisman français très célèbre.	He's a famous French tennis player.
C'est le meilleur footballeur du monde.	He's the best footballer in the world.
Elle a gagné la médaille d'or aux jeux Olympiques.	She won the gold medal at the Olympic Games.
Elle a battu le record mondial.	She beat the world record.
Ils sont champions du monde.	They are the world champions.
Il est vedette de cinéma.	He is a film star.
Elle a eu un succès fou en Suède.	She had a wild success in Sweden.
La France va gagner la coupe du monde.	France is going to win the World Cup.
Il a perdu en demi-finale.	He lost in the semi-finals.
L'Italie a battu l'Irlande.	Italy beat Ireland.

QUELQUES PAYS

l'Afrique	Africa
l'Allemagne	Germany
l'Amérique	America
la Belgique	Belgium
le Canada*	Canada
le Danemark*	Denmark
l'Espagne	Spain
les Etats-Unis**	United States
la Grèce	Greece
l'Italie	Italy
les Pays Bas**	Netherlands
le Portugal*	Portugal
la Suisse	Switzerland

to/in = en
BUT
* to/in = au   **to/in = aux

LES LANGUES

le danois	Danish
le flamand	Flemish
le grec	Greek
le hollandais	Dutch
le portugais	Portuguese

Au Québec on parle français

Il y a beaucoup de problèmes.	There are lots of problems.
Le problème le plus grave, c'est la pollution.	The most serious problem is pollution.
Il faut conserver l'énergie.	We have to save energy.
J'essaie de ne pas consommer d'essence.	I try not to use petrol.
Je vais au collège à pied.	I walk to school.
Les voitures émettent des gaz toxiques.	Cars give off poisonous fumes.
Je suis écologiste.	I am an ecologist.
Au collège, il y a des papiers partout.	At school, there is paper everywhere.
C'est affreux.	It's disgusting.
Il faut protéger les animaux sauvages.	We have to protect wild animals.

QUESTIONS/PROMPTS

Vous avez visité les autres pays de l'Europe?
Vous voudriez aller aux Etats-Unis? Pourquoi?
Parlez-moi de votre chanteur préféré.
Que faites-vous pour protéger l'environnement?

LES STARS

un acteur/une actrice	actor/actress
un(e) chanteur/se	singer
l'équipe (de France)	the (French) team
un groupe	group
un(e) guitariste	guitarist
un(e) joueur/se	player
un présentateur/une présentatrice	presenter/announcer

CHECK YOURSELF QUESTIONS

Q1 How would you say this in French?

A I went to the Netherlands last year.
B The most important city is Amsterdam.
C All the Dutch can speak English.
D Next year I will go to Africa.
E I'd like to go round the world.

Q2 Which country is it?

A La capitale est Berne.
B Elle se trouve au sud-ouest de la France.
C Une des plus grandes villes est Edimbourg.
D On y parle flamand et français.
E Elle était divisée en deux parties, est et ouest.

Answers are on page 161.

On devrait utiliser l'énergie du vent.
Nous devons essayer de conserver les ressources naturelles.
Dans cinquante ans, il n'y aura plus de pétrole.
Les gaz carboniques émis par les véhicules sont très dangereux.
Il y a plus de maladies respiratoires.

Un autre problème, c'est les CFC émis par les bombes aérosol.
L'atmosphère, les océans, les rivières, sont tous pollués.
Nous laissons des ordures partout: les papiers, les sacs en plastique, même les déchets nucléaires
Il faut essayer de sauver les espèces en danger.

We should use wind power.
We ought to try to save natural resources.

In 50 years there will be no more oil.
The carbon gases produced by vehicles are very dangerous.
There are more respiratory (breathing) illnesses.

Another problem is the CFCs produced by aerosols.
The atmosphere, the oceans, the rivers, are all polluted.
We leave our rubbish everywhere: paper, plastic bags, even nuclear waste.

We must try to save endangered species.

L'ENVIRONNEMENT	
l'atmosphère	atmosphere
le climat	climate
l'eau	water
l'effet de serre	the greenhouse effect
la pluie (acide)	(acid) rain
la pollution des eaux	water pollution
le recyclage	recycling
le réchauffement de la planète	global warming
le trou dans la coucho d'ozono	the hole in the ozono layor

LES SOURCES D'ENERGIE	
l'énergie solaire	solar power
l'énergie nucléaire	nuclear power
l'énergie des vagues	wave power
l'hydro-électricité	hydro-electricity
le pétrole	oil

Il y a certains éléphants qui sont en voie de disparition.
Les zoos protègent les animaux sauvages.
Si la population continue à augmenter, il y aura encore des famines.
On peut facilement recycler le papier et le verre.

Certain elephants are becoming extinct.

Zoos protect wild animals.
If the population continues to grow, there will be more famines.
One can easily recycle paper and glass.

LES PROBLEMES	
la drogue	drugs
la faim	hunger
la pauvreté	poverty
la sécheresse	drought
la soif	thirst

These are very wide topics, and you will not be expected to discuss them in the same detail as you might in English. However, at Higher Level, you will be expected to be able to say a couple of sentences about major world issues such as pollution, the environment and conservation, and to understand simple discussions or newspaper articles about them.

? Check Yourself Questions

Q1 Fill in the missing word.

A On peut utiliser l'_____ des vagues.

B Il ne reste plus beaucoup de _____.

C Il faut essayer de _____ l'énergie.

D On doit utiliser le vélo plutôt que la _____.

E A la maison, nous recyclons toutes nos _____.

bouteilles	papier
énergie	vent
pétrole	conserver
sauver	voiture

Q2 What are they talking about?

A On n'a pas eu une goutte de pluie depuis le mois de février. C'est un vrai problème.

B Il y a trop de personnes au Tiers-Monde qui n'ont pas assez à manger. C'est une honte.

C Si on continue à les tuer comme ça, ils vont disparaître.

D Il faut interdire les bombes aérosols – sinon, on ne pourra plus sortir au soleil.

E Les plages et les rivières deviennent de plus en plus dangereuses. On ne peut pas se baigner sans risques.

la pollution des eaux
la sécheresse
les espèces en danger
la pluie acide
la pollution de l'atmosphère
la surpopulation
la faim

Answers are on page 162.

REVISION SESSION 3 ▰ How the grammar works ▰

🥖 Relative pronouns

■ The relative pronouns *qui/que* and *ce qui/ce que* have been dealt with in Unit 6. There is, however, another set of relative pronouns which are usually used with prepositions.

■ Like most pronouns, they change according to the gender of the noun to which they refer:

lequel (masculine singular)	*laquelle* (feminine singular)
lesquels (masculine plural)	*lesquelles* (feminine plural)

J'ai un cahier dans lequel j'écris tous mes devoirs.	I have a notebook in which I write all my homework.
Il y a de petites tables sur lesquelles elle a mis des plantes.	There are some little tables on which she has put plants.

■ They can be used as one-word answers to questions:

Tu me passes un stylo, s'il te plaît?	Will you pass me a pen, please?
Lequel?	Which one?

🥖 Indefinite adjectives, adverbs and pronouns

■ *Autre* is used in a number of different ways:

Tu as une autre jupe?	Do you have another dress?
J'ai un disque de Vanessa Paradis. Je voudrais les autres.	I have one record by Vanessa Paradis. I'd like the others.
C'était pas moi. C'était quelqu'un d'autre.	It wasn't me. It was somebody else.
Entre autres.	Among other things.

■ *Quelqu'un/quelque chose* mean 'someone' and 'something':

Je voudrais te présenter quelqu'un.	I'd like to introduce you to someone.
J'ai quelque chose à te montrer.	I have something to show you.

■ *Tout* has a number of different uses:

J'ai mangé toute la glace.	I've eaten all the ice-cream.
Il a vu tous les films de Depardieu.	He's seen all Depardieu's films.

(Note the irregular masculine plural).

Il les a vus tous.	He's seen them all.

(Note that, when used in this way, the final *-s* is pronounced.)

- *Tout* is also used in a number of common expressions:

tout le monde	everybody (always singular in French)
tout de suite	straight away
tout à fait	completely
tous/toutes (les) deux	both

CHECK YOURSELF QUESTIONS

Q1 How would you say this in French?

   A Where are the others?

   B Have you lost something?

C Everybody is happy.

D He broke all the records.

Answers are on page 162.

REVISION SESSION 1 — ◼ How to overcome problems ◼

🔊 Problems and solutions

In some ways, it is impossible to separate the four skills. To understand and use French, you need to know **the vocabulary**, and to know **how the structures work**. This is as true when you are reading French as when you are listening to it. However, there are some ways in which listening is different. Listed below are some of the general problems associated with listening. You can help yourself to overcome them mainly by practising.

Problem 1
When you are listening, the French is gone after the second hearing, and you can do nothing to bring it back (whereas when you are reading, you can simply look back at the previous paragraph).

Solution
The Listening Test in the French exam isn't like most of the listening you do. Most of your everyday listening (music on the radio, the conversation of your friends, even sometimes school assembly!) is no more than a background to some other activity. In your Listening Test, you really need to concentrate on what you hear. You can practise concentrating on listening in very short bursts – even a TV soap can be useful. Listen for five minutes (time yourself), then try to write down as much detail as you can of what you heard. If you can record it, then play it back to check, so much the better. Obviously, you need to practise listening to French as well, so ask to borrow a cassette from your teacher – almost anything will do. What you are trying to do is to build up your power to concentrate on what you hear.

Problem 2
Distractions can be much more important when you are listening. There isn't much you can do about low-flying aircraft, but it is all too easy to drift off into a day-dream, and completely miss a sentence or two.

Solution
This is clearly linked to Problem 1. If you don't often listen to anything in a concentrated way, you probably never concentrate on listening for a long period, which you need to do in your Test. Again, you need to practise, but this time it's easier with your teacher's help. Ask him/her to make sure you do some practice on past papers, so that you have an idea of how long you will need to concentrate for. Also, perhaps even more than for any other sort of test, you need to be fresh. Everyone will tell you this is true for all your exams (and so it is) but if you are in any danger of nodding off, the Listening Test will surely encourage you to do so – and of course it's absolutely fatal!

Problem 3

The speakers in the Test may have regional accents, and would therefore sound very different from your teacher. There will also be both male and female voices, which you may not be used to in French.

Solution

If your school has a French *assistant(e)*, or any native-speaker teachers, take advantage of them to get used to different voices and accents. Similarly, if there are any French exchange students in your school/area, listen to them.

Problem 4

It's more difficult listening to someone you can't see, as you don't have the benefit of gestures, lip movements and so on.

Solution

Get as much practice as you can in listening to tapes, to get used to having no visual clues. Even try closing your eyes sometimes in French lessons – as long as the teacher doesn't think you've fallen asleep!

Problem 5

There may well be sound effects recorded (from traffic noises to echo effects like the telephone) which come between you and the meaning of what you hear.

Solution

The sound effects in Listening Tests shouldn't be too off-putting – in fact they are usually meant to help you, to put what you hear in some sort of context. Try to make use of them.

Using the question to help you

■ When the question is a simple factual one it will often tell you exactly what information you are listening for, for example:

> *Une glace coûte: 1,15€   15€   1,25€   1,75€   ?*

You know that you are listening for a number, and you can ignore any other information you hear.

■ The question will still help you if it is less simple, but still factual, for example:

> *Une glace à la vanille coûte: 1,15€   15€   1,25€   1,75€   ?*

Here, you have to put the price and the flavour together, but once you have got the cost of a vanilla ice-cream, that's all you need.

■ If the question is about an emotion or an attitude, there are certain kinds of word you should listen for, for example:

> *Myriam aime l'anglais: VRAI   FAUX   ?*

You might listen for words like:

> *ennuyeux/difficile/préférée/intéressant/passionnant,* or phrases like *le prof est sympa/je ne suis pas forte.*

What you probably won't hear is *j'aime* or *j'adore* – that would be too easy!

Using the context to help you

■ For example, you might hear the following:

> *Derrière la maison, il y avait un vieux chêne. Quand il était petit, il s'installait dans les branches pour regarder les voisins dans le jardin d'à côté.*

You may not know that *un chêne* is an oak tree, but the context should make it fairly clear that it's a tree of some sort.

Using your common sense

■ If you know that someone is in a hotel, he/she is more likely to say:

> *Vous avez une chambre pour une nuit?*

than:

> *Vous avez des oignons?*

You have acquired some knowledge of France and the French way of life, so make use of it. You should know that an ice-cream is more likely to cost *1,50€* than *15€*.

🥖 Numbers

- These are often tested at Foundation Level (in times, prices and so on) and even at Higher Level they can form an important element of a number of answers. Ask your teacher, or the French *assistant(e)*, or a friendly 6th form French student, to record some numbers for you to practise listening to.

- Remember that the numbers in context often sound different from the numbers you practised when you were in Year 7. *Deux* on its own has one sound (*deuh*) but it can sound very different before a word beginning with a vowel (*deuz enfants*). This can be a real comprehension problem – try comparing *deux enfants* and *douze enfants*. The only sound difference is the vowel sound (*eu* and *ou*). Similar problems occur with *trois/treize*, and *six/seize*.

- The other difficulty with French numbers comes in the numbers between 70 and 99. Again, lots of specific practice in listening to numbers is the answer. Try practising particular times and telephone numbers, where you are likely to hear a combination of several numbers: *quinze heures cinquante-trois* (15.53); *le zéro-quatre, soixante-sept, quatre-vingt-huit, onze, quatre-vingt-quatorze* (04, 67, 88, 11, 94).

🥖 The alphabet

- The spelling out of certain words, especially names and places, is quite common over the telephone.

- Particular problems can be caused by:
    E (euh – as in the word *deux*) and I (ee – as in the English word 'peep')
    B (bé) and P (pé)
    D (dé) and T (té)
    G (jé) and J (jee) (both with a soft *j* as in the French word *je*)
    H (ash)
    M (emm) and N (enn)
    Y (ee grec)

See also Unit 15: Speaking, page 95.

✑ Consonants

- Any pronunciation practice you have done has probably been mainly concerned with vowel sounds. While it is true that French vowel sounds can be quite difficult for an English speaker to produce, they don't often lead to confusion in listening, except in some numbers and some letters of the alphabet (see page 80).

- It can be much harder to hear the difference between some consonant sounds, and the problem is greater because either way can result in real French words. Try to get a recording of some odd-one-out exercises based on consonant differences, for example:

    bain   pain   bain   bain

    Other easily confused consonants are *m/n*; *d/t*; *f/v*.

✑ Negatives

- These are very easy to miss, and yet are vitally important to understanding. Indeed, their whole purpose is to change the meaning of a sentence.

- In colloquial speech, the problem is even greater, since the *ne* is quite often omitted. Again, try some odd-one-out listening exercises:

    je l'ai vu   je l'ai vu   je l'ai pas vu   je l'ai vu

✑ Language patterns

- These are much easier to make use of in reading, but it is worth noting the different ways the French can spell the same or a similar sound, so that you can try various alternatives for a sound you don't recognise:

    -ant, -ent, -end, -and, -an, -en, -amp, -anc at the end of words all have the same sound.

    -ez, -é, -ait, -aient all sound the same or similar, and are all verb endings.

- Do some listening practice where you try to distinguish between these spellings simply on the basis of grammar:

    A   *Il regardait le journal.*
    B   *Vous regardez le journal.*
    C   *Elle a regardé le journal.*

    This is only partly a listening exercise, but it will help put together sounds and structures, which is a very important part of listening for meaning.

Word separation

- This is really what listening problems are all about. In reading, you can identify the words by the white space on each side. In listening, all the words are often run together. It can be hard to use your knowledge of vocabulary if you can't distinguish the words.

- The only solution is lots of listening practice, aided by a variation on an old-fashioned technique called dictation. Take a recording of almost any piece of French which is at, or a little below, your level – taken from your course-book, for example – and try to write down what you hear, using clues like intonation and natural pauses, to help you identify the words. Of course, one of the most important clues is the meaning: you will recognise lots of the words, and this will help you to pick out the unknown ones. If you have a transcript of the recording, you can check how well you did. Don't forget, the object of the exercise is to distinguish the individual words rather than to spell them right, but it's almost equally valuable without the check, since it's doing the exercise that matters.

Higher Level performance

At Higher Level, you will be expected to be able to do a number of things which are not expected at Foundation Level.

Understanding French spoken at normal speed

At Foundation Level, especially for Grades E, F and G, the speakers will slow down a little – as a French person would, knowing he/she was speaking to a foreigner. At Higher Level, the speakers will speak more naturally – though not at the very rapid rate they might use to their friends. Speakers are also more likely to use colloquial expressions and even some slang (understanding of this will not be tested), and to use the contracted forms common in everyday speech, for example *J'sais pas, moi* instead of the more formal *Je ne sais pas, moi*.

Extracting information from longer utterances

Here, it's not that the information is more difficult, but that you have to pick out what is relevant from a longer item. For example, at Foundation Level, you might be asked to identify the weather from a sentence like:

> *Demain, il fera beau.*

At Higher Level, you might hear an extract from a weather forecast:

> *Demain, dans le nord-est du pays, il fera assez froid. Dans le sud, il fera beau, et dans l'ouest, il y aura des orages.*

You might then, for example, be asked to identify the weather in the south. In each case, the French targeted by the question is the same (*il fera beau*), but at Higher Level you have to understand more of the context in order to get there.

Picking out the main points from what you hear

You might listen to a discussion on going out, in which three people make a number of different points but all say how important the cost is – in different ways. One might say:

> *Ça doit coûter au maximum cinq euros.*

Another might say:

> *Le problème, c'est que les discothèques sont souvent trop chères.*

The third might say:

> *Ça dépend du prix d'entrée.*

You need to identify the fact that they are all concerned about the cost.

Identifying attitudes and opinions

This does not mean just understanding words like *heureux*, *content* or *ennuyé*, but understanding that when someone says *Franchement, pendant les cours d'histoire, je m'endors*, this implies that they are bored.

Making deductions from what you have heard

As a simple example, if you hear:

> *Il a plu tous les jours. La tente était toute mouillée.*

you can deduce that the speaker has been camping.

Understanding the gist of what you hear

If you hear someone say:

> *Il y a tant de problèmes aujourd'hui. On manque d'eau potable dans plusieurs régions du monde. Puis il y a la pluie acide qui menace les arbres, et les gaz toxiques qui menacent notre santé.*

you can put all that together and identify that they are concerned about the environment.

Answering questions using French which you have not heard

You may have to answer questions in phrases or sentences that are not simply repeating what you have heard. In the previous example, if you were given the question:

> *Quelle est l'attitude de Jean?*

you would have to reply with (for example):

> *(Il pense qu') il y a des problèmes d'environnement.*

Giving any of the individual details (lack of drinking water, acid rain, poisonous gases) would not score the mark.

Understanding vocabulary outside the minimum core vocabulary

Each board defines a minimum core vocabulary for Foundation Level. This would normally be the vocabulary which you need to carry out the tasks specified in the syllabus, though there will certainly be words in the Listening Test which you have not met. One of the Higher Level skills is to use your linguistic skills to fill in any blanks in vocabulary. Just as in English, if someone uses a word you don't know, you can still follow the gist of what they are saying. Obviously, the more words you know, the better your understanding will be, but understanding is not simply a matter of knowing the words.

Different kinds of listening

Listening for detail

Start from the question. Decide whether the word(s) you are listening for is, for example, a time, a price, a place or an object, etc., and concentrate on listening for that.

Listening for gist

If the question is more general, asking for someone's feelings or opinions, or asking 'what sort of...?', individual words and phrases are less important. What matters is the whole message. In some ways this kind of question is more difficult, but at least it is less important if there is a word that you don't understand.

Dialogues

If the question asks you to link different views or opinions to different people, it is very important to keep track of who is speaking. The names of the speakers will be clearly recorded. In an interview, the interviewer may introduce each speaker by name:

> *Qu'est-ce que tu en penses, Joël?*

In a conversation, the speakers will refer to each other frequently by name:
> *Moi, je préfère les maths. Et toi, Lucie?*

In this sort of question, the name will always be printed on the question paper, so you don't need to worry about recognising unfamiliar names. Quite often, the question will ask you to write the name (or the initial) of the person who expresses a particular view:

> *... pense qu'il va devenir professeur*

or to complete a grid by putting the correct information next to each person's name.

Monologues

These are more likely to be factual. Possible examples include: radio news bulletins, weather forecasts, advertisements, guides to tourist attractions and recordings of pen-friends. The question will make it clear who is speaking, so keep this in mind when you are answering the questions.

✎ Announcements

These are mainly at the lower levels, and may include: announcements in shops, stations, airports, etc.; public address announcements (on the beach, in town, on a boat, etc.). The questions will often target dates, times and prices.

✎ Telephone calls and recorded messages

Again, these will often target dates and times, with perhaps the added complication of a change in arrangements. In this last case, you will have on the question paper details of, for example, an appointment. As you listen to the message, you need to compare what is written with what you hear, and note any differences.

There are four basic question types, but there are a number of possible variations within each.

✎ Multiple-choice (in pictures) _____

In this kind of question, you simply have to choose the picture which best fits what you hear. There will usually be four pictures to choose from, lettered or numbered, and you write down the appropriate letter/number. Sometimes, there may be six or more pictures to accompany several questions. For example, you might see six pictures lettered A to F, each representing a job. You will then hear four recordings in which a person describes the job he/she wants to do. For each person, you choose a letter A to F.

1   The pictures may be symbols (icons), for example, a stethoscope to represent a nurse, or a plane to represent an airport. Your exam board may have a set of such symbols. Make sure you know them.

2   They may be numbers (clock faces, calendars, prices, etc.).

3   They may be more general pictures to represent a more complicated idea, for example, a beach scene with the sun and people playing volleyball.

The first two types of picture will usually give a factual detail which you need to listen out for. The third will probably relate to the gist of what you hear. It may be important with this sort of picture to make sure that all the details fit with what you have heard – in other words, that if the speaker talks of a beach holiday playing volleyball, but spoilt by the weather, you do not choose the picture with the sun on it! However, the pictures will never be all that complicated, and any detail differences will be very clear.

✎ Multiple-choice (in words) _____

There are a number of types, in increasing order of difficulty:

1   One-word answers. Typically, these will be filling in blanks, often at the end of a sentence:
    Marie est _____ . [contente/ennuyée/fâchée/triste]

    In simpler questions of this type, the missing word will be one that you hear; in more complicated questions, you will have to work out which of the words offered fits best.

2   Phrase answers. These are similar to one-word answers:
    Elle va vous rencontrer _____ . [à la gare/au café/à l'hôtel/au cinéma]

3   Sentence answers. These are usually more difficult, and can take two forms.

Either:

Pourquoi est-ce que Jacques est content?

A *Il adore l'anglais.*

B *Il a réussi à son examen d'anglais.*

C *Il a passé son examen d'anglais.*

D *Il aime le prof d'anglais.*

Or:

Choisissez la bonne personne pour chaque phrase:

– *est bon élève*

– *travaille seulement quand il aime la matière*

– *n'a pas fait grand-chose à l'école*

– *espère devenir professeur*

In this type of question, it is important that you understand **exactly** the meaning of the sentences offered.

Answers in French

Again, the answer can consist of one word, a phrase or a whole sentence.

1 One-word answers. These will often ask you to fill in a form or a grid. Spelling will usually only be taken into account if it gets in the way of communication, but you do need to take care. For example, *collage* (a very common error) is only one letter different from *collège*, but since the mistake creates a real French word, it is a big problem for communication. The word required for the answer will often be one you have heard on the recording.

2 Phrase answers. These are more complex than the multiple-choice phrase answers, since not only do you have to produce the correct key word, but the rest of the phrase will also need to be appropriate. For example, in answer to the question:

Où vont-ils se rencontrer?

the answer *café* is not clear enough. You would need *au café* (or maybe *devant le café*) to make yourself understood, and to score the mark.

3 Sentence answers. These will only appear in the most difficult questions (Grades B and A), as they require you not only to understand what you have heard, but to be able to manipulate the language in order to reply. This may simply be a question of adapting what you have heard on the recording. For example, you have heard someone say:

Je suis forte en maths.

In your answer you have to say:

Elle est forte en maths.

However, you may sometimes have to create a whole sentence for yourself. For example, the question is:

Des jeunes parlent de leur ville. Quelle est l'attitude de Claire?

You hear Claire say *Il y a pas mal de choses à faire – le cinéma, les discothèques, le théâtre.*

You need to answer *La ville est intéressante* or *Il y a beaucoup de distractions*, etc.

✑ Answers in English

Though these may seem to be the easiest, they will often be used to test the most difficult items, and the most difficult kinds of understanding. They will frequently be used to test your understanding of the gist of longer items, or your ability to draw conclusions from what you hear, or identify opinions and attitudes. Don't assume that you can simply pick out key items of vocabulary. The question is often looking for more than this. These questions will often contain the words 'How?' or 'Why?' or phrases such as 'What was X's reaction?'

Questions to try

Find Unit 14: Questions to try on the CD (Track 1). Listen to each item twice, then answer the questions.

1 A l'hôtel, vous avez demandé l'heure du dîner.
Le dîner est à quelle heure? Cochez la case appropriée.

A de 7h00 à 9h00 9   **C** de 7h00 à 9h30 ☐
B de 7h30 à 9h00 ☐   **D** de 7h30 à 9h30 ☐   [1]

FOUNDATION

2 Qu'est-ce que vous devez faire quand vous quittez l'hôtel?
Cochez la case appropriée.

A prendre la clé à la réception ☐
B laisser la clé à la réception ☐
C le dire à la réception ☐
D emporter la clé ☐   [1]

FOUNDATION + HIGHER

3 Vous écoutez la météo. Indiquez le temps sur la carte.
Ecrivez une lettre dans la case appropriée.

FOUNDATION + HIGHER

A 13°   D   E 16°
B   C   F

i ☐ ii ☐ iii ☐ iv ☐   [4]

4 Karine, qu'est-ce qu'elle préfère comme vacances?

HIGHER

Cochez la case appropriée.

A ☐   **B** ☐   **C** ☐   **D** ☐   [1]

5 Ecoutez l'annonce. Indiquez les **deux** phrases qui sont vraies. Cochez **deux** cases.

A Si vous achetez vos billets au syndicat d'initiative, ils sont moins chers. ☐

B Si vous achetez vos billets à l'entrée, ils sont moins chers. ☐

C L'annonce concerne un cirque étranger. ☐

D Le spectacle commence à neuf heures. ☐

E Il y a beaucoup d'animaux au cirque. ☐ [2]

HIGHER

6 Ecoutez ce message téléphonique. Corrigez les erreurs.

MESSAGE TELEPHONIQUE	
POUR:	Mme Lucas
DE LA PART DE:	M. Dupuis
MESSAGE:	Rendez-vous à l'hôtel de ville à 6h15

[3]

HIGHER

7 Ecoutez ces conversations, puis choisissez le mot qui convient pour chaque personne. Ecrivez **J** (Jeanne) ou **A** (Amélie) dans la case appropriée.

réservé(e) ☐   sérieuse ☐

enthousiaste ☐   timide ☐

égoïste ☐   [2]

HIGHER

8 Où était le camping? Complétez la phrase.
Le camping était _____ [1]

HIGHER

9 Où étaient les parents? Complétez la phrase.
Les parents étaient _____ [1]

HIGHER

10 Julien, pourquoi veut-il aller à l'université? [1]

HIGHER

11 Hélène, pourquoi a-t-elle décidé d'étudier les maths? [1]

HIGHER

12 ANSWER IN ENGLISH.
M. Blanchard is talking about his family's recent holiday.

A Name two of the problems they had at the hotel. [2]

B Why could M. Blanchard not solve the problems? [1]

C What was the result of one of the problems? [1]

D (i) How did they finally feel about the holiday? [1]

   (ii) Why? [2]

HIGHER

[Total: 25 marks]

You will find the transcripts and answers, with examiner's comments, on pages 163–5.

UNIT 15: EXAM PRACTICE
SPEAKING

How to overcome problems

✍ Problems and solutions

This unit concentrates on the specific skills and techniques which will enable you to perform at your best in the Speaking Test. There are three possible parts to the Speaking Test. Role-plays and General Conversation are common to all the exam boards; the Presentation is used by OCR and AQA (Specification A) only.

Unlike in listening, where you have no control over the language used – you simply respond to what other people say – in speaking you always have some room for manoeuvre.

In the role-plays, there are often slightly different ways of saying the same thing, and you need to choose the one which you are most comfortable with.

In the General Conversation, you have some freedom of expression in responding to what your teacher says, but you also have a great deal of choice about the content. You can choose how much to say in response to any question, and you can select the information that you decide to include.

Finally, if your exam board includes a Presentation in the Speaking Test, you have total choice about the topic and language you use.

Here are some general problems which are specific to speaking, with some possible strategies for overcoming the difficulty, or getting round it.

Problem 1

One of the major difficulties many candidates find in the Speaking Test is overcoming their nerves. Even the most outgoing personality can be reduced to a nervous wreck as soon as he/she is faced with a microphone. One reason for this is that, unlike in any other exam, your teacher is actually there with you – and will notice every silly mistake you make.

Solution

Before the Test – in fact from the beginning of the course – practise speaking French onto a cassette. When you are asked to prepare a role-play, or any other piece of oral work, don't just do it in your head, get out your cassette recorder. In this way, not only will you get used to being recorded, you will have a record of what you have done, and you'll be able to go back and listen again in the light of your teacher's comments. When it comes to the day itself, try to relax. A really deep breath as you go into the exam room will help, as will taking a few seconds to settle yourself comfortably and arranging your papers before you start.

Problem 2

The temptation is to rush the parts you have prepared, before you have time to forget! This can not only spoil your pronunciation and intonation, but it can also lead to you making errors that you wouldn't otherwise make.

Solution

When you are making your practice recordings, make sure you speak steadily and clearly. No-one will expect you to speak as quickly as a native French speaker at this level. You are still in the position of needing to think about intonation, and sometimes about some pronunciations, so don't let your desire to get it over with let you down.

Problem 3

However, speaking steadily does not mean hesitating after every other word. This will spoil your pronunciation just as much as rushing, and will also be taken into account in the marking.

Solution

There are two sorts of hesitation. The first, when you've been asked a question in the Conversation and need to think about the information you're going to give – your favourite film, for example – is perfectly natural, and nothing to worry about. The second sort of hesitation, which you should avoid if possible, is when you are searching for a word in French. It shouldn't happen in the Foundation or Foundation/Higher role-plays, which you should have prepared thoroughly in advance. If it happens in the Higher role-play, where you can't always predict exactly what's coming, or in the Conversation, you can try to conceal it – with 'noises' like *euh...* , or phrases like *Je ne sais pas.*

Problem 4

Sometimes, however, there is no way of concealing either that you can't answer a question, or that you haven't understood the question. It is very easy, when this happens, to simply allow the conversation to grind to a halt, and it can then be quite hard for you and your teacher to get it going again.

Solution

The important thing here is to let the teacher know as precisely as possible what the problem is, so that he/she can take appropriate action to keep the conversation moving.

- If the problem is that you don't understand what you've been asked, say so as clearly as possible. If it's a general problem, you can say *Je ne comprends pas* or *Voulez-vous répéter, s'il vous plaît.* This should result in the teacher either repeating the question – probably a little more slowly – or re-phrasing it slightly in the hope that you will then understand it.

- If the problem is simply that you don't understand one of the words in the question, you could say *Je ne comprends pas* (French word) or *Que veut dire* (French word)?, in which case the teacher will try to explain, so that the conversation can continue in the same direction.

- If the problem is that you can't remember a word you need for your answer, you could say *J'ai oublié le mot pour* (English word), in which case the teacher will tell you, and the conversation will continue as above.

These last two techniques will not gain you any credit for the words you didn't know, but they will allow the conversation to flow fairly naturally.

Don't just sit there in silence. This makes it hard for your teacher, who doesn't know whether you are just pausing for thought or whether you're really stuck, and will therefore hesitate to move on. This will make the conversation sound very stumbling, and will also waste time.

Problem 5

You may be allowed to make notes when you are preparing the role-plays. If a Presentation is part of the Speaking Test, you may be allowed to make notes or cue-cards. You will be able to take these with you into the exam room.

Solution

Whatever form these written notes take, try not to read them out. Reading aloud is a skill on its own, and most candidates are not very good at it – it affects their intonation and pronunciation very badly.

- For the role-plays, you should use the notes:

  1 to make sure that you know exactly what you are going to say (for the Foundation and Foundation/Higher role-play).

  2 in the exam room (if this is allowed), as a back-up, in case your mind suddenly goes blank.

- For the Presentation, you should use the cue-cards simply to keep your ideas in order, as a guide to the sequence of what you are going to say. Some candidates make their cue-cards in visual form, just to avoid the danger of being tempted to read aloud.

Without using a special alphabet, it is difficult to describe the sounds which are made by particular letters. One way is to compare the sounds with words which you certainly know – in English where there is a close match, otherwise in simple French words. The other way is to model your pronunciation on that of a native French speaker. The first part of the CD for Unit 15 (Track 2) contains most of the French sounds you are likely to need. Listen to the CD while you follow this list of words. In the printed list, the sounds being practised are in bold.

A	**ma**			N	**noir**	
B	**bar**			O	**mot**	**port**
C	**car**	**cette**		P	**père**	
D	**dix**			Q	**qui**	
E	**le**	**mère**	**fête** **mangé**	R	**reste**	
F	**faux**			S	**sa**	
G	**gant**	**âge**		T	**ta**	
H	**habite**			U	**sur**	
I	**si**	**fin**		V	**vin**	
J	**je**			W	**wagon**	
K	**kilo**			X	**fax**	
L	**la**			Y	**Sylvie**	
M	**ma**			7	**zéro**	

AI	**maison**		OI	**soir**	
AU	**au**		OU	**sous**	
EI	**reine**		UI	**huit**	
EU	**heure**	**deux**			

AN/EN	**dans** **dent**		AIN	**bain**	
IN/IM	**instant*** **impact***		EIN	**hein**	
ON	**mon**		OIN	**coin**	
UN	**brun**				

*BUT if the consonant is doubled, pronunciation is much more like the English: *immédiat*; *innocent*.

∾ Vowels

As you can see from the above, vowels have a number of different sounds, depending on which other letter(s) they are combined with, or, in the case of E, on the use of accents. When used on its own:

- **a** is pronounced as in the English word 'man'.
- **e** is pronounced as in *de*.
  é is pronounced as in *clé*.
  è and **ê** are pronounced as in *mère*.
- **i** is pronounced as in the English word 'peep'.
- **o** is not like any English sound.
- **u** is not like any English sound.

✏ Consonants

Although French consonants are not pronounced in exactly the same way as English consonants, the differences are not usually enough to cause any real problems. However, here are a few tips:

- **c** is pronounced like 's' before *e* and *i*, but like 'k' before *a*, *o* and *u*.

- **g** is pronounced 'soft' (i.e. as in *je*) before *e* and *i*, but 'hard' (as in the English 'gun') before *a*, *o* and *u*.

- **h** is completely silent in French, though it can affect the sound of other letters, as in *château* and *pharmacie*.

- **q** sounds like 'k', as in *qui*.

- **r** is probably most easily produced by rolling the tip of the tongue against the roof of the mouth. Don't worry too much about it, as long as you make sure it can be clearly heard.

- **w** is pronounced like 'v'.

- **x** is usually pronounced like 'ks', as in *fax* (but is usually silent at the end of a word).

- **y** is pronounced like the French *i*.

- **z** is usually pronounced like 'z', as in *zéro* (but is usually silent at the end of a word).

Probably the most useful thing to remember about consonants in French is that, if they come at the end of a word, they are not usually pronounced, unless the next word begins with a vowel. For example:

- *Vert* is pronounced as if it did not have a *t* at the end, but in *verte* you can clearly hear the *t*.

- The sentence *Ils regardent la télé* sounds exactly the same as *Il regarde la télé*. (The *-ent* plural ending on verbs is always silent.)

- However, in the sentence *Ils entrent dans la cuisine* you can hear the *s* on *Ils* since it's followed by a vowel.

The alphabet

You are quite likely, in one of the role-plays, to be asked to spell out someone's name or the name of a place. Listen to the next section of Unit 15 on the CD (Track 3) and learn the sounds of the French alphabet. Make sure that you can spell out your own name, and any family names (especially if they are very different from French names) and the place where you live. Practise recording these onto your own cassette.

An approximate guide to the pronunciation of the letters of the alphabet is given below, for quick revision.

A	a as in 'man'	O	o as in *mot* (no English equivalent)
B	bé		
C	sé	P	pé
D	dé	Q	ku (no English equivalent of *u* sound)
E	eu as in *deux*		
F	eff	R	airr
G	jé	S	ess
H	ash	T	té
I	ee as in 'jeep'	U	u (no English equivalent)
J	ji (almost) as in *jupe*	V	vé
K	ka	W	dooble-vé
L	ell	X	eeks as in 'peeks'
M	emm	Y	ee-grek
N	enn	Z	zed

If a word contains a double letter, say *deux* followed by the letter:

```
... ss ...    = deux ess*
... pp ...    = deux pé
... rr ...    = deux airr*
```

* The *x* is heard but it sounds like a *z*.

Verbs

One of the most common mistakes in the Speaking Test is to pronounce all verbs, especially *er* verbs, as if they end in *é*. This makes it impossible for the person you are talking to, to work out whether you are speaking in the past (perfect or imperfect) or the present, since *je mangé* could be a mistake for *Je mange*, or *j'ai mangé*, or even *je mangeais*. This would lead to a lot of confusion, and possible misunderstanding, so would have a serious impact on your accuracy mark. Practise making it absolutely clear whether you are saying:

> *Je mange à la cantine.* (I have lunch in the canteen.)
> *J'ai mangé à midi.* (I ate at twelve o'clock.)

or even:

> *Je mangeais quand le professeur est entré.* (I was eating when the teacher came in.)

How to tackle role-plays

Role-plays are used by all exam boards. In most cases, candidates who are entered for Foundation Tier will do the Foundation role-play and the Foundation/Higher role-play, while candidates entered for Higher Tier will do the Foundation/Higher role-play and the Higher role-play.

The OCR Higher role-play is slightly different from the others, in that it asks the candidate to relate a series of events, rather than take part in a dialogue.

Candidates are given 10–12 minutes to prepare the role-plays.

The boards will use symbols, such as a question mark (**?**) to tell you that you should ask a question, or an exclamation mark (**!**) to tell you that you should answer the teacher's question.

In the instructions for the role-plays you might meet the following phrases:

C'est à vous	You should	*Donnez*	Give
de commencer	begin	*Epelez*	Spell
Choisissez	Choose	*Expliquez*	Explain
Commandez	Order	*Payez*	Pay
Décrivez	Describe	*Proposez*	Suggest
Demandez	Ask for	*Répondez*	Answer
Dites	Say	*Saluez*	Greet

Check your own specification to know exactly what you should expect.

Foundation

The tasks will be presented in English, either as a paragraph or as separate instructions, accompanied by visuals.

Preparation

- Rehearse in your mind what you will say for each of the four or five tasks.

- Remember that the instructions tell you what the task is. You do not have to translate them into French. For example, if the instruction says: 'Ask your friend what time he gets up', you only need to say *Tu te lèves à quelle heure?*

- The teacher will start the role-play unless otherwise stated.

- If you are allowed to make notes, do so, but don't be tempted to read a script.

- Don't spend too long on the preparation. You will need more time for the Foundation/Higher role-play.

In the test

- Be calm. You will have the instructions with you, so you don't have to remember what to do.

Foundation/Higher

At this level, there will always be an unpredictable task, i.e. one that is not specified on the candidate's card for you to prepare in advance. The scene will be set in English, and there will be either visual or verbal prompts for each task. The verbal prompts may vary from single words to full-sentence instructions in French, depending on the board.

Preparation

- Check any vocabulary you need and go over in your head what you will say for each of the tasks.

- Work out where the unpredictable element comes, and try to work out what it might be. For example, if you are telephoning to book a hotel room, you will probably be asked your name. If this is not one of the specified tasks, there's a good chance it might be the unpredictable one.

In the test

- Remember that you can only handle the unpredictable task if you understand what the teacher is asking you. You need to listen carefully.

Higher

These role-plays will always contain a problem to solve or something to negotiate. The exception is the OCR Higher role play, where the candidate must give an account of a series of events.

Preparation

- You really need to think yourself into the situation at this level, so that you can respond naturally however the situation develops.

- You can't write yourself a script in advance, since so much depends on what the teacher says.

- All you can do is to try to predict what sort of problem might arise, and make sure that you plan ways to cope.

In the test

- The main thing is to respond appropriately to what the teacher says, so again, listen carefully.

- Be sure to make all the points mentioned on the candidate's card, even if you have to go back over something.

Higher (OCR)

Remember that you are giving an account, so you must use the past tense.

Preparation

- Make sure you say something about every picture. You don't have to mention every detail, but they give you an idea of how much you should say overall, and if you can't think of any other details, you should probably make use of those suggested.

- Make sure you give full accounts, with descriptions and link words. Don't stick to the bare minimum.

In the test

- It's really a question of remembering what you've prepared. You will have the candidate's card to remind you, so it's not just a memory test. You will also need to respond to what your teacher says.

How to tackle Presentation and Discussion

Presentation and Discussion forms part of the Speaking Test for OCR and AQA Specification A only, though similar tasks may be done as part of the Coursework option with Edexcel.

Both boards require you to speak for 1 minute (OCR) or 30–90 seconds (AQA) on a topic of your choice taken from one of the areas of experience. The teacher will then ask you some questions about your Presentation.

Choosing your topic

You could choose a very familiar topic, such as *Ma famille*, or *Mon école*. You could be more independent, and talk about *Mon passe-temps préféré*, or you could decide to talk about *Mes vacances en Italie* or *L'échange scolaire*. The choice is yours, but do discuss it with your teacher, because your choice can affect the mark you get.

- If you choose a 'basic' topic, you may end up only demonstrating a limited amount of the French that you know. It would be very easy, for example, to talk about your school using short, familiar sentences, giving few opinions, and entirely in the present. If you are in fact able to express opinions clearly, and to refer to the past and the future, this would certainly restrict your grade.

- If you choose an obscure topic (for example, if your hobby is bell-ringing!), you need to do a lot of work on the vocabulary.

- Make sure that your teacher knows in advance what your Presentation is going to be about. This will give him/her the chance to plan some intelligent and helpful questions.

- Make sure that your first sentence says what the Presentation is about. Your teacher might know, but the examiner listening to you on cassette won't, unless you say so.

How much detail

You should include enough detail to make it interesting, but not so much that it becomes tedious. The main idea is to show off your knowledge of French.

- Try to avoid lists of vocabulary. For example, if you are talking about your hobby, give two or three of the key bits of equipment you need. If you are talking about your school, you don't need to list all the science labs one by one or give the names of all the teachers.

- Try to avoid using English words. If your Presentation is about *La télévision*, talk about the programmes in general terms – say *J'aime les feuilletons* (I like soaps), then give an example, rather than *J'aime EastEnders*. If you are talking about *La musique* say *J'adore les groupes anglais* rather than *J'adore Oasis*.

- It is possible with almost any topic to say something about the past and the future, as well as the present. Even an unpromising topic like *Mon uniforme scolaire* can produce sentences like *A l'école primaire, je ne portais pas d'uniforme* and *Dans les écoles de l'avenir, il n'y aura pas d'uniforme.*

Cue-cards

These are vital to keep what you are saying in order, and to stop you 'drying up'.

- Keep them to short phrases, or even key words.

- Don't have too many, otherwise you risk getting them mixed up.

- Number them, just in case you drop them on the floor just before the exam!

- Don't read from them (see Problem 5 on page 94).

- Although you may have written a script to give you confidence while practising, you will not be allowed to read from it, as it's against the rules. In any case, it would ruin your pronunciation.

Delivery

You should practise thoroughly, preferably recording yourself on cassette.

- You don't need to learn your Presentation off by heart (it's probably better if you don't, as you will sound more natural, and run less risk of 'forgetting your lines'), but when you go in to the exam you should know pretty well what you are going to say.

- Don't rush; speak clearly and steadily, without too much hesitation.

- Your practice should include timing. This will give you a good idea of whether you've got too much detail.

- Many of the topics lend themselves to the use of photographs and other visual aids, for example, if you are talking about a holiday, or your family. However, don't have too many, and don't just restrict your Presentation to a description of a series of photos:
  Voici mon père. Voici ma mère. Voici la plage. Voici notre hôtel.

  It could get very dull, and doesn't allow much opportunity for demonstrating a range of language.

Predicting the questions

It's a good idea not to include every bit of information, so that you leave the teacher something to ask you. For example, if you are describing a holiday, and don't mention the accommodation, it's fairly certain that the teacher will ask about it.

- The teacher will not be trying to catch you out, but to encourage you to develop further what you have said.

- He/She will probably stick to the well-tried questions: 'What?'; 'Where?'; 'When?'; 'Who with?'; 'Why?'; 'How much?' 'How long?'

How to tackle General Conversation

General Conversation is common to the Speaking Tests of all the exam boards. You will be expected to carry out a conversation with the teacher on a variety of topics from the specification (they may be chosen by the teacher, or at random, or you might have some choice). In some specifications, some topics are only available at Higher Level. You need to check the precise requirements of your board.

The main thing to remember about the General Conversation is that it is your chance to show off what you know. There is no point in knowing four tenses and having an enormous vocabulary if you don't use them.

Tenses

You must make sure that you refer to past, present and future events during the Conversation. Your teacher will ask you questions aimed at encouraging you to use different tenses – it's up to you to respond.

- Listen out for *tu as* or *tu es* (+ past participle), and when you hear it, make sure you answer in the past – *j'ai* or *je suis* (+ past participle).

- If the teacher asks you a question containing *tu vas* (+ infinitive), reply in the future with *je vais* (+ infinitive).

- It is important to note that if you don't refer to past, present and future, you will not get a Grade C!

Opinions

Have some ready-made expressions for expressing different opinions – not just the basic *j'aime/je n'aime pas/j'adore/je déteste*, but more complex ideas such as:

Je crois que	I think that
Il me semble que	It seems to me that
A mon avis	In my opinion
Je (ne) suis (pas) d'accord avec	I (don't) agree with
J'ai horreur de ça	I really hate that
J'en ai marre de	I'm sick of

Again, without expressing opinions, you won't get a Grade C.

Full accounts and descriptions

In the General Conversation, you are rewarded for the range of your language. To score well you need to include:

- some longer sentences, linked with words like *mais*, *alors*, *puis*

- some sentences containing *qui* and *que*

- a variety of adjectives and adverbs

■ extra details, without being asked. In other words, if you are asked a question like *Tu as des frères ou des sœurs?*, you can launch into a description of them without waiting for any further questions:

> *Oui, j'ai une sœur. Elle s'appelle Marie. Elle est plus âgée que moi – elle est à l'université où elle étudie les langues.*

What not to do

Since the examiner can only assess what **you** say:

■ Don't allow long pauses to develop.

■ Don't let the teacher say more than you do.

■ Don't hesitate before every word.

■ Don't force the teacher to drag every word out of you. Volunteer some information.

■ Don't be embarrassed to have a go. It doesn't have to be perfect to communicate.

 Role-plays

For each role-play, spend a few minutes working out what you would say –
and for the Foundation/Higher and Higher role-plays, trying to predict what
the teacher might ask. You should probably spend about two minutes on a
Foundation role-play, about three minutes on a Foundation/Higher, and five
to six minutes on a Higher.

Find Unit 15: Questions to try on the CD (Track 4). Listen to the
sample student's answer and compare it with your own.

1 You are at a leisure centre in France.

- Say which sport you want to play.
- Say how many there are of you.
- Ask how much it is.
- Say how long you want to play for.

Your teacher will play the part of the assistant and will speak
first.

FOUNDATION

2 You are in a café in France. You want to buy something to drink
and to eat. Say what you would like to drink, say what you would
like to eat, ask where the telephone is and end the conversation
politely.

FOUNDATION

a You would like **one** of the drinks below.

b Say what you would like **to eat**.

c Ask where the telephone is.

3 You are talking to a French friend about your part-time job. You will have to:

- say where you work (e.g. in a shop)
- say from 5 till 9 o'clock
- say on Monday
- say four pounds.

Your teacher will play the part of the friend and will start the conversation.

4 You have lost something in France, and go to the lost property office to enquire about it. You will have to:

- say what you have lost (e.g. your case)
- reply to a question
- say where you lost the item
- say when you are going home.

Your teacher will play the part of the assistant and will start the conversation.

5 You arrive at a French hotel. The examiner will begin the conversation.

a Say what sort of room you want.

b Answer the question.

c Say how many nights it is for.
d Ask what time breakfast is.

6 SITUATION: The notes and pictures below give an outline of a day spent in Normandy. Tell the examiner what happened. You need not mention every detail, but you must cover the whole day's events.

Be prepared to respond to any questions or comments from the examiner.

ARRIVER

Manger le petit déjeuner

Quel temps?

où?

Décider de faire du shopping

DES ACHATS

Qu'est-ce qu'on a acheté?

coûter combien?

LA VISITE

château?

cathédrale?

musée?

intéressant?   ennuyeux?

L'APRES-MIDI

plage   –   avec qui?

jouer

pique-nique

LE SOIR

restaurant

mangé?
bu?

discothèque

dormir

quelle heure?

7 While you are in France you feel unwell, and go to see a doctor.

- Symptômes.
- Depuis quand?
- **!**
- Départ demain?

When you see this – **!** – you will have to respond to something you have not prepared.

Your teacher will play the part of the doctor, and will speak first.

8 You have applied for a job in a French restaurant.

The examiner will play the part of the manager and will begin the conversation.

> **RESTAURANT** LE MANOIR
> recherche
> SERVEUR/EUSE
> été 2003

a Raison pour travailler en France.
b **!**
c Heures de travail?
d **!**
e Salaire?

Presentation and Discussion

You should only do this if your exam board has it as part of the Speaking test. However, it would do no harm to listen to the CD – it might give you some useful ideas about things you could say about your family.

Prepare a presentation of about 1½ minutes about your family. Then, in Unit 15: Questions to try on the CD, find Track 5 and listen to the sample student's answer. Did you say the same sort of things? Did you manage to fit in a variety of tenses and structures? Did you anticipate the questions the teacher was likely to ask?

General Conversation

First listen to the questions which begin this section on the CD (Track 6), and answer each one as fully as you can. The topics covered are House and Home, Leisure and Education and Future Career. Give lots of detail, and don't forget that if the teacher asks a question in the past or the future, you should make sure that you use a verb in the past or in the future in your reply. Then listen to the sample student's answer, and compare it with your own.

You will find transcripts of the sample answers, with examiner's comments, on pages 166–71.

How to overcome problems

Problems and solutions

Reading is generally thought to be the easiest of the four skills. It is certainly true that, when reading in their own language, people can almost always understand more than when listening, and much more than they can actually produce in speech or writing. However, there are some particular problems with reading.

Problem 1

Some of the material you are asked to read in the exam might be handwritten. Handwriting is always more difficult to read than print, and it can be even more so in a foreign language. In addition, French handwriting is quite different from English handwriting, and this can cause problems with recognising letters, which can lead to comprehension difficulties.

Solution

Make sure that you have seen some examples of French handwriting before the exam. You or a friend might have a French pen-friend, or there may be a French teacher at your school. You will be able to pick out the letters which you find hard to read, and so be prepared to meet them in the exam.

Problem 2

Because it is 'easier' than listening, passages in the Reading Test, especially at Higher Level, tend to be longer and more dense. This has implications for timing, as well as for understanding.

Solution

There are several strategies for dealing with a long text, some of which will be looked at later in this chapter, but one of the most important is to approach the text in the right way. You should always begin by reading through the whole passage to get the gist. You should then approach a detailed understanding via the questions. Usually, questions will be asked in the order that the information appears in the text. In other words, once you have found the answer to Question 1, the answer to Question 2 will appear later in the text. There may be exceptions to this, particularly when a question is asked about the gist of part of, or the whole, passage, but it is still a reasonable starting point.

Problem 3

You are much more likely to meet words that you do not know in reading than in the other skills.

Solution

Again, some of the strategies for coping with unknown words will be looked at later in this chapter, but the main thing is not to panic. You may not need to understand the word at all in order to answer the question.

Problem 4

Written language tends to be more formal than the spoken language, and to use more complex structures. In particular, you may meet two parts of the verb which you will probably not use, or meet in speech, and which you might have met rarely, if at all, in class. These are the past historic tense, which has the same meaning as the perfect tense but is found almost exclusively in literature and journalism, and the subjunctive, which is used in certain phrases, usually after *que*.

Solution

You will find a reference to these in the Further Grammar section but generally, for the purposes of reading, you simply need to recognise which verb they belong to. This is usually fairly easy – it's just a question of removing the ending and seeing what's left – though there are one or two irregular verbs where it's a bit more difficult.

Problem 5

Because you have more control over reading than over listening, the questions often require closer attention to detail, since you can move about a text and go back to the beginning very easily in a printed passage.

Solution

Try to work systematically, studying a section at a time, and possibly ticking it when you think you have all the information. It's very tempting to jump about from paragraph to paragraph looking for a particular word or phrase, but you risk repeating what you have already done, and missing out just the part where the answer is.

✐ Coping with unknown words

Learning vocabulary

In Reading (and Listening) the majority of marks are lost by candidates because they do not know a particular word or phrase. Therefore, the more words you know, the better your mark.

■ When you are reading a passage for homework or in class, keep a dictionary handy. You won't need to look up every word you don't know (see pages 110–11) but if you look up just a few each time you read a passage, some of them will stick.

- Learning words 'by accident' is a lot easier (and often a lot more effective) than trying to learn a list of vocabulary. Try these tricks:

  - When you look up a word in your dictionary, look at the word before and the word after. If you need to look up a job, for example, look up another word in the same category. You don't have to make an effort to learn them, but you will remember some of them.

  - Find a friend who also wants to acquire some new vocabulary, and turn it into a game: who can produce the longest list of buildings/ who can be first to produce five fruits beginning with 'p'? You'll know some of the words, but you'll have to look some up to win!

  - If you have to learn a list of words (for example, for a test at the end of a topic), again turn it into a game. Arrange the list in alphabetical order, in pairs (opposites for example) or in order of length: anything, in fact, which turns the hard slog of learning into fun. Not only will you get better marks in your test, but the words will also stick for longer.

How to tackle a passage

- Read the instructions and the questions first.

- Read through the passage to try to get the gist.

- Try to match up the questions with the appropriate paragraph or section of the text.

- Look out for key words that might tell you where the answer is: numbers (as in dates, times, prices) can often pinpoint where you should look.

- Answer as many questions as you can.

- By now, you should know roughly where in the passage the missing answers are to be found. In these areas, try to apply the **Strategies for understanding**.

- If none of this helps, use the context and apply your common sense. For example, in the sentence *Il n'y avait pas de trains hier à Paris à cause d'une grève*, there aren't that many reasons for there being no trains, so a (sensible) guess stands a reasonable chance of being right (in fact *grève* means 'strike').

✍ Strategies for understanding

There are many ways of understanding words that you have never met, without using a dictionary, but instead using grammatical markers and word patterns and similarities. The more of these strategies you can use, the more you will understand.

Verbs

If you are familiar with the various forms of verb endings, it will be easy enough to remove the ending, and get back to the stem of the verb, which can often be enough to enable you to identify it. For example, if you read *nous dînions*, you will know it's a verb. Remove the ending and you are left with *dîn...* . The infinitive is probably going to end in -*er*, giving *dîner*. Even if you have never met it as a verb, you can easily work out its meaning by comparing it with the familiar noun *le dîner*.

Adjectives

If you are familiar with irregular feminine and plural forms, you can again often get back to the stem of the word. For example, *nationaux* is much easier to understand if you know that *-aux* is the way in which words ending *-al* make their plural.

Nouns

Again, familiarity with irregular plural forms can save a lot of time struggling to work out what an 'unknown' word means.

French word patterns

■ If *re-* is added to the front of a verb, it means the action is being done again: *revoir* – to see again.

■ The ending *-erie* on many shops is well known, but less known is the ending *-er* or *-ier* to refer to someone who works in such a shop: *boucher*; *épicier*.

■ The addition of *in-* (or *im-* before *b*, *m* or *p*) to the front of an adjective reverses its meaning, so *mangeable* means 'edible', *immangeable* means 'inedible'.

■ The ending *-aine* added to numbers turns it into an approximate or round number: *une dizaine* – about 10.

French/English word patterns

■ French nouns ending in *-té* often match English nouns ending in '-ty': *beauté*.

■ French adverbs ending in *-ment* often match English adverbs ending in '-ly': *complètement*.

■ French present participles ending in *-ant* often match English present participles ending in '-ing': *entrant*.

■ French words which have a circumflex accent often match English words which have an 's': *forêt*.

■ French words which begin with *dé-* often match English words which begin with 'dis-': *décourager*.

■ French words which begin with *é-* or *es-* often match English words which begin with 's-': *espace*.

Similar words in English and French

These are far too many to list, and there are of course some which are 'false friends'. For example, *journée* has absolutely no connection with 'journey' – it means 'day'; and *un car* doesn't mean 'a car', but 'a coach'. However, it is certainly worth trying to make use of these similarities. If you are reading a passage in French and you come across a word which (within a letter or two) is the same as an English word, then try to fit it in the context. If it makes sense, then assume it's right.

At Higher Level, you will be expected to be able to do a number of things which are not expected at Foundation Level.

Understanding a variety of types of writing

■ Authentic extracts from magazines and newspapers. These will include long and complex sentences, and a significant proportion of words which are not in the Minimum Core Vocabulary. These will not be tested, but you will need to be able to use the context, or one of the strategies referred to above, to help you understand the gist of the passage.

■ Letters – either printed or in authentic handwriting – which include long sentences, unknown words, and possibly colloquial expressions.

■ Extracts from fiction. These will be reasonably short, but may include structures such as the past historic and the subjunctive.

■ Advertisements, where the message is not always explicit, and you need to deduce the answer.

Picking out the main points and themes

If a question is aimed at the theme or the main point of a passage, an answer which gives specific details will not score very highly, and may not score at all.

■ This type of understanding is often tested through English. So if you read an article about a play, which says that the acting was bad, the dialogue was unconvincing and the sets were ridiculous, and you are asked what the author thought of the play, 'He didn't like it' – although it seems vague – is actually a better answer than 'The acting was bad'.

■ Picking out the main point involves a similar technique, but is often tested through multiple-choice in French. So in an article about the environment, the author might include sentences such as: *Il faut utiliser moins les voitures; Nous devons tous éteindre la lumière quand nous quittons une pièce; On doit tenir fermées les portes et les fenêtres.* You might then be asked to choose the most suitable of the following sentences.

L'auteur pense que le problème le plus important, c'est:

A *le prix de l'électricité*
B *la conservation de l'énergie*
C *le manque de pétrole*
D *le chauffage domestique*

All of these appear in the article, but only **B** could be counted as the most important problem.

Identifying attitudes and opinions

As in listening, this is not a question of seeing and understanding words like *ennuyé* or *agacé*, but of interpreting that someone who says that she shouted at her brother when he borrowed her make-up was annoyed.

Making deductions from what you read

This is a question of reading a sentence like *Quand elle est rentrée au bureau, elle était toute bronzée* and deducing that she had been on holiday.

Answering questions using French which is not in the passage

If you read *Après le collège, je n'ai pas l'intention de continuer mes études, je préfère travailler*, you might be asked to complete the following sentence:

Elle va chercher _____

None of the words in the printed sentence will fit; you need to put *un emploi* OR *du travail*.

▰ Different kinds of reading ▰

✑ Skimming

This is particularly useful when you have a lot of text with a small number of quite specific questions – or even a single question. For example, you may have a series of short letters to a magazine, and you need to say which writer fulfils a certain requirement.

- You may simply need to look through each letter to find a single word. For example, if the question is *Qui parle anglais?*, you may just need to skim through each letter to find the word *anglais*.

- You may need to find a certain category of word. For example, if the question is *Qui parle trois langues?*, you need to skim through each letter looking for words for languages, and note (don't trust to memory – write it down) the number you find for each person.

- You may need to find one detail for each person, and compare them. For example, if the question is *Qui est le plus jeune?*, you need to skim through each letter and note (again, write it down) the age of each person, and then select the youngest.

The important thing to remember in this type of question is that you are looking for a specific piece of information, and you can ignore everything else. In this type of question it is usually not necessary to read the passage first – you can go straight to the question.

✑ Reading for detail

This is rather similar to skimming, but the questions may be a little less specific, or there may be a number of questions of detail about a single medium-length or long text. In order to find where in the passage the answer comes, it is useful to identify a key word.

- This may be something as precise as a number (time, date, etc.). For example, if the question is *Le voyage a duré combien de temps?*, you are clearly looking for a length of time, which will probably involve a number (though think of other possibilities too, such as *une demi-heure*, *une journée*).

- The key word might be a little less precise. If the question is *Le voyage était...* a) *très bon?* b) *pas mal?* c) *mauvais?*, you need to find the place in the passage where the word for 'journey' appears – though of course the word might be *trajet* or *traversée*, for example, as well as *voyage*.

Remember that almost always in this kind of question, the answers will appear in the passage in the same order as the questions appear on the paper. It is useful here to read the passage through quickly before studying the questions, so that you have an idea of the overall meaning – it can save time if you know which bits of the passage contain which ideas.

✍ Reading for gist

This is often the most difficult sort of reading, since you really do need to have a good overall understanding of what you read, though it is not necessary to understand every detail. This sort of item will often have questions in English.

■ You may be asked to identify someone's attitude:
Michèle est contente de sa vie de famille.   *VRAI?*   *FAUX?*

What Michèle says may include good and bad things about her family life, and you have to put everything together and come up with a decision based on the balance of what she says.

■ You may be asked to identify the main point or theme of what you read. This may not be stated explicitly; you may have to deduce it from what is written.

It is important here to read the passage right through carefully, but at this stage don't worry about words that you don't understand. Ideas are often repeated in different ways, and understanding a particular word may not matter at all.

✍ Using the text layout to help understanding

Extracts from newspapers/magazines
■ Headlines in large print will tell you what an article is about.

■ Articles are often divided into paragraphs. If these have a sub-heading, again this will help with the gist. The paragraphs can also help to pinpoint a particular sort of information in a particular section.

■ **Bold** print and *italics* are often used to draw attention to important points or key ideas.

■ The photographs in an article, although they won't give away the answer to any of the questions, will give a clue to what the article is about.

■ Figures, charts and tables are often used. Their purpose is to give information simply and clearly to the reader, but they can work for the candidate too.

Notices and advertisements
■ Like newspaper articles, these make use of changes in print size to draw attention to particular information, and to separate one category of information from another. For example, opening times will often be in a different type-face from, for example, the address. This can help you, if you are looking for specific information.

■ The use of centering, bullet points, etc. is also used to highlight certain pieces of information.

Letters

- Letters in French have more or less the same layout as letters in English, so the top right-hand corner will tell you where the letter was written, and the part at the end before the signature will simply be the closing greeting.

- If you are finding the handwriting difficult, it sometimes helps if you find a word that you do recognise, and compare the way the letters in that word are written with a word that you can't work out.

REVISION SESSION 4 ▬ Different kinds of question ▬

There are four basic question types, but there are a number of variations within some of them.

✑ Multiple-choice (pictures)

The aim is to choose the picture which best fits a word, a sentence, or a paragraph.

- Single vocabulary items. In these, you might have, for example, a list of jobs and a series of pictures illustrating certain jobs, and you have to link each picture to the right word.

- A similar technique can be used to test a number of vocabulary items together. For example, you might read: *Dans mon sac, il y avait mes clés, ma carte de crédit, et un flacon de parfum*. You then have four pictures of bags, showing different contents:

  A a ring, keys and a credit card
  B perfume, credit card and keys
  C credit card, perfume and 50€
  D keys, perfume and a diary

  The only choice which matches is **B**.

- The picture might be more general. For example, you read about someone's holiday, and have to decide which fits best:

  A a beach scene   C a country scene
  B a mountain scene   D a hiking scene

- A variation on this is a series of pictures to be put into the correct order according to what you read. At Foundation Level, this might take the form of a separate account (for example, of a day in the country), followed by a series of pictures which you have to put in order. At Higher Level there might be a story from a picture magazine, including speech bubbles which are printed out of order, and you have to note the correct order. If you find this kind of exercise difficult – and you may do, no matter how good your French – it might be a good idea to leave this question until last. It can take a long time to sort out. However, if you do decide to leave this, or any other question, to be done later, make sure you go back to it, even if you only have time to more or less guess at the answers. You should never leave an answer blank, especially if it's just a question of choosing the correct letter or box to tick.

✑ Multiple-choice (words)

Again, there are a number of types.

- One-word answers. These may take the form of an English sentence, followed by a number of one-word items (such as shop names) to choose from. For example:
     Where do you go to buy bread?

  A BOUCHERIE   B BOULANGERIE   C CHARCUTERIE   D GARAGE

At a higher level, you may be given a passage with blanks, and you have to choose from a list which word fits which blank. In this sort of exercise, there will often be more words in the list than there are blanks. A variation on this is a complete passage, followed by a series of sentences, each with a blank which you have to fill with a word from the original passage. When you are choosing words to fill a blank, it is often useful to know whether you are looking for a verb, an adjective or a noun.

- If the blank comes after a subject pronoun (*je*, *tu*, *elle*, etc.) it must require a verb.

- If the blank comes after a definite or indefinite article (*le/la/les* or *un/une*) it probably requires a noun.

- If the blank comes between an article (see above) and a noun, it must require an adjective.

■ Phrase or sentence answers. Often, these take the form of a number of sentences following a passage, of which you have to choose (by ticking or writing a letter) the two or three which are correct according to the passage.

✍ Answers in French

Like the above, this can consist of one word, a phrase or a sentence in French. There will often be an example to show how long an answer is expected.

■ At Foundation/Higher Level, the answer will often be largely taken from the text. For example, in a letter, you might read: *J'ai un frère.* One of the questions might be: *Elle a combien de frères?* The expected answer would be: *Elle a un frère.*

■ You might be asked to fill in a form – for example, with personal details, or details of lost property.

■ At Higher Level, you may be asked to construct a sentence of your own to answer a question, but this will not usually require more than a fairly simple sentence, drawing on vocabulary from the original passage.

✍ Answers in English

These are often used to test the most difficult ideas, and at Higher Level will almost certainly want more than simple details based on vocabulary.

■ Open questions in English at Higher Level will often ask 'Why?', 'How?', 'In what circumstances?' or 'What difference?', and will test either gist understanding, or understanding of a complex idea or sentence.

■ Multiple-choice answers in English may be used to test gist, or detailed understanding of a large section of text.

1   You want to catch a train. Which sign should you follow?
    Tick ONE box only.

    A ☐ PISCINE >   B ☐ GARE SNCF >

    C ☐ BIBLIOTHEQUE >   D ☐ GARE ROUTIERE >   [1]

FOUNDATION

2   Answer the questions in English.

    LA PETITE FERME

    entre Villeneuve et St-Maurice

    ouverte à tous les enfants de 3 à 13 ans
    de 10h à 18h
    fermée le lundi

    lapins, chèvres, moutons, volaille

    Oui, tu peux toucher!

    A Who is **La petite ferme** for?   [2]
    B When is it closed?   [1]
    C What are visitors allowed to do?   [1]

FOUNDATION

3   Regarde ces objets.

    A   B   C

    D   E   F

    Où est-ce qu'on les trouve? Ecris la lettre dans la bonne case.

    CHAMBRE ☐   CUISINE ☐   SALON ☐   [6]

    JARDIN ☐   SALLE DE BAINS ☐ SALLE A MANGER ☐

FOUNDATION

4 Lis la lettre et réponds aux questions.

Chère Dominique,

Je suis enfin arrivée en France, après un voyage atroce. La mer n'était pas du tout calme, et j'ai été malade. En plus, il y avait beaucoup d'enfants qui ont crié toute la nuit.

Le père de ma correspondante m'attendait au port, et m'a emmenée en voiture. Il a l'air assez sympa, sa femme aussi, et Nathalie est tout à fait comme dans ses lettres – très ouverte et bavarde. Je sens que je vais m'amuser avec elle.

L'inconvénient, c'est la situation de leur maison. Elle se trouve assez loin des autres maisons mais elle donne sur la route nationale, alors il y a de la circulation jour et nuit. Tu sais, je n'ai pas l'habitude, car j'habite dans un coin assez tranquille. La nuit dernière, je n'ai pas dormi.

Heureusement, la semaine prochaine, je vais partir à la mer avec la famille, et ils m'ont dit que la villa qu'ils ont louée n'est pas sur la route. Je l'espère!

Grosses bises
Amélie

Coche (✔) la bonne case.

A Le voyage a été…

bon ☐   assez bon ☐   mauvais ☐

B Amélie est…

contente ☐   assez contente ☐   pas contente ☐
de la famille.

C La maison se trouve…

en ville ☐   près d'une ferme ☐   dans un village ☐

D La semaine prochaine, Amélie espère…

aller à la plage ☐   rentrer à la maison ☐   bien dormir ☐

[4]

5 Regarde ces extraits des lettres de quelques jeunes Français et Françaises.

> **Julie**
> Moi, j'ai trois frères et deux sœurs. D'habitude ça va, mais je n'aime pas partager une chambre avec ma petite sœur. Il n'y a pas beaucoup de place.

> **Alexandre**
> Chez moi, il y a seulement mes parents et moi. C'est bien, car ma mère me gâte, mais quelquefois je voudrais un frère ou une sœur pour jouer avec.

> **Aurélie**
> Je sors souvent avec ma sœur. Elle a deux ans de plus que moi, mais elle me parle comme à une amie, elle me prête ses vêtements et ses disques. C'est bien.

Qui dit quoi? Coche (✔) la bonne case.

	Julie	Alexandre	Aurélie
Je suis fils/fille unique.			
Je m'entends bien avec ma sœur.			
J'ai une assez grande famille.			

[3]

6 Lis cet article.

> ◆　**Beso – génie à 11 ans**　◆
>
> Il a sa propre exposition dans une galerie à Londres. Il a déjà créé plus de 3 000 tableaux. Rien d'étonnant peut-être – mais à 11 ans?
> Ce petit gamin géorgien peint depuis l'âge de 4 ans. Encore rien d'anormal, car tous les enfants aiment la peinture. Mais le directeur de la galerie d'art, Roy Miles, est convaincu qu'il a trouvé un vrai génie. Il a découvert l'artiste lors d'une visite en Géorgie.
> Beso n'est pas d'une famille riche – tout au contraire – et comme tous les enfants de son pays il a connu la guerre et la violence. C'est ce qu'il peint!

Coche (✔) les trois phrases correctes.

A Beso est un artiste superbe. ☐
B Il a quatre ans. ☐
C Il est pauvre. ☐
D Ses tableaux sont exposés en Géorgie. ☐
E Les tableaux représentent les problèmes de son pays. ☐ [3]

7

PROJETS D'AVENIR

Voici la réponse de Martine:

En ce moment, ça va pas mal à l'école, mais on verra après les examens l'année prochaine. Je voudrais faire des études supérieures – de préférence des études de commerce. Puis j'ai envie de travailler à l'étranger pendant quelques années, avant de m'installer en France et mener une vie de famille.

Mon rêve serait de trouver un emploi dans une grande entreprise, et de passer un an en Italie, un an en Belgique et deux ou trois ans aux Etats-Unis. Heureusement, je parle assez bien anglais, et j'ai habité pendant trois ans à Rome, alors je parle couramment italien.

Pour finir les phrases, choisis parmi les expressions **A** à **F**.
Puis écris la bonne lettre dans la case.

I Après le lycée, Martine voudrait... ☐
2 Elle n'a pas encore envie... ☐
3 Elle a l'intention... ☐
4 Elle n'aura pas... ☐

A ...de se marier.
B ...de problèmes avec les langues étrangères.
C ...d'enfants.
D ...de travailler dans plusieurs pays différents.
E ...travailler en Europe.
F ...continuer ses études. [4]

8 Ecris le nom de la personne.
Tiphaine, Olivier et Sandrine parlent de la fête du cinéma, qui a lieu les 29, 30 juin et 1er juillet.

Tiphaine, 21 ans: J'y vais une fois par semaine. Ça dépend de ma bourse et de mon temps. Pendant la fête, je compte voir au moins 5 films, car pendant ces trois jours, on paie le premier film à plein tarif, et après on ne paie que 10 francs par film.

Olivier, 21 ans: Je vais au cinéma, bien sûr, mais pas de façon régulière. Si j'ai des examens, j'y vais pas. En général, j'y vais deux fois par mois. Les places sont tellement chères que je ne peux pas me permettre d'y aller trop souvent.

Sandrine, 20 ans: Pour moi, le cinéma, c'est un plaisir qui me permet de tout oublier et de changer de vie pendant deux heures. J'y vais tous les samedis, et assez souvent en semaine aussi. Ça change de la monotonie quotidienne et c'est une façon de se cultiver.

A Qui n'a pas assez d'argent pour aller souvent au cinéma?
B Qui trouve que les films sont un moyen d'éviter la réalité?
C Qui va profiter de la fête pour voir beaucoup de films?
D Normalement, qui va le plus souvent au cinéma? [4]

9 Read this article, then answer the questions in English.

Vos papiers, s'il vous plaît!

Depuis 1993, la situation des 'sans papiers' en France est très difficile. Il s'agit d'immigrés qui sont en France depuis des années, et qui avant cette date auraient eu le droit d'y vivre. Mais ils sont maintenant considérés comme clandestins, et leur statut est illégal.

Pour protester, et pour demander leur régularisation, ils ont trouvé asile dans l'église St-Bernard à Paris.

Le cinquante-deuxième jour, la police a forcé les portes de l'église. A l'aide de brutalité physique et de gaz lacrymogène, les policiers ont mis fin à la résistance.

La question des immigrés joue un rôle de plus en plus important dans la politique française. Le Front National profite de la peur que ressentent beaucoup de Français face au chômage et aux problèmes sociaux des grandes villes.

Arif, lui, vit à Paris. Ce n'est pas un immigré – il est né en France, et il se considère comme français. "Les gens ont peur de ceux qui ne sont pas comme eux" dit-il. "S'il y a du chômage, c'est à cause des immigrés. Si les gens sont agressés dans la rue, c'est à cause des immigrés. Ce qu'ils ne disent pas, c'est que ce sont les immigrés qui sont les plus touchés par le chômage, et que les victimes des agressions, ce sont très souvent des immigrés."

HIGHER

Line 10: *statut* = status
Line 13: *asile* = asylum
Lines 18/19: *gaz lacrymogène* = tear gas

A How has the position of immigrants without papers changed since 1993?

B What happened to end the asylum of the group of immigrants in St Bernard's Church?

C Why is the National Front attracting more voters?

D What is Arif's response to accusations that immigrants are responsible for unemployment and street violence?

E How would you describe the general tone of the article? [5]

[Total: 34 marks]

You will find the answers and examiner's comments on pages 172–3.

REVISION SESSION 1

How to overcome problems

🍞 Problems and solutions

This unit deals with the skills and techniques you will need to help you gain maximum credit in the most difficult of the language skills.

Most people find the accuracy needed to score highly in writing quite hard to achieve. If you have studied the topic-based chapters of this book thoroughly, you will have acquired all the structures you need to achieve a very high mark in writing. However, it is not only accuracy that counts. You also need to express ideas and opinions, and to give full and detailed accounts.

As in speaking, however, you do have one great advantage. There is always some choice of content, and therefore of language, in the Writing Test. Some boards actually give you a choice of question in the Writing Test. If this is the case for you, make sure you choose wisely. Don't spend too long on the choice, but don't simply go for the first option. Look at the topics, and ask yourself which one you feel happiest with. Do you know a lot of vocabulary in that topic? Do you have some ready-made phrases which would fit? Even if the paper set by your board doesn't give you any choice of question, you can still to some extent choose what to say.

Here are some of the problems which are specific to writing, with some suggestions as to how you might overcome them or avoid them.

Problem 1
Understanding the question.

Solution

Make sure that you are familiar with the layout of the Writing paper set by your own board. The general pattern will remain the same from year to year, and in particular the early questions will ask for similar things every year. However, in the later questions, and at Higher Level, you must make sure that you understand what you have to do.

Problem 2
Deciding what you want to write.

Solution

There are a number of golden rules here.

- Don't start by working out in detail in English what you want to say, and then putting it into French. You will always end up trying to say things you have never learnt, you'll get the structures wrong and what you write may not make sense.

- Don't be in too much of a rush to get started. Many candidates aim to finish in time to make a 'fair copy' of what they have written. This is usually a bad idea. You often end up simply copying the mistakes you made in the first draft (because you don't really have time to write all your answers twice), and adding a few new ones too as you rush to get finished.

■ It's much better to start by making a plan. This needn't take long, nor be too full, but it will help you to know where you're going. If the question gives you a series of tasks to do (in French or in visual form), make a note – at this stage in English if you like – of what each task is, and of some useful words and phrases (in French). If your task is to reply to a French prompt, such as a letter which asks a number of questions, jot down in English the questions which are asked, and then list some useful French words and phrases.

Problem 3
Deciding how much to write.

Solution
Most boards actually suggest on the question paper the number of words you should write, and you should obviously follow these suggestions. AQA does not specify a number of words, but at Foundation Level, Question 2 will require about 35 words, and Question 3 about 90 words, while at Higher Level, Question 1 will require about 90 words, and Question 2 about 120 words. For all boards, what really matters is carrying out the specified tasks, so you shouldn't spend too long counting the words, and if you find you've written a few words over the 'limit' you should certainly not spend ages trying to cut them out. However, if you write much less than the suggested number of words, you will probably lose marks.

Problem 4
Producing accurate work.

Solution
Unfortunately, there is no easy answer to this. However, there is one thing you can do to minimise inaccuracies, and that is to check your work. Simply reading over what you have written is not likely to highlight many mistakes, but a structured approach can really help. Try to leave yourself enough time at the end to go through the following check-list:

1 Make sure that verbs agree with their subject. Common errors are to put a singular ending after *ils* or *elles*, (often putting -*e* instead of -*ent*, or -*ait* instead of -*aient*). If you're in a hurry, you can at least check that after *tu* your verb ends in -*s* (it always should), and after *il/elle/* someone's name, the verb does not end in -*s* (it never should – perhaps -*t*, -*d* or -*e*, but never -*s*).

2 Make sure that all your perfect tense verbs have the correct part of *avoir* or *être* as well as the past participle. The commonest verb error of all is to write, for example, *je parlé* instead of *j'ai parlé*.

3 Check that if you've used an adjective with a feminine or plural noun, you've made the adjective feminine or plural too.

Problem 5

Completing all the tasks. If you forget to do one of the tasks – even one of the simple ones like the greeting at the beginning of a letter, or the ending of a letter – you will lose marks for content, and this might even affect the other marks for that question too.

Solution
Either on the question paper, or on your plan, tick each task as you do it. This makes it less likely that you'll leave one out.

✎ Making use of the French that is on the paper

Clearly, you are not going to get any credit for simply copying phrases or sentences from a letter or an advertisement which is printed on the question paper. However, the material is there to help you, and as long as you change or adapt it in some way, it becomes your language, and will be marked accordingly.

- Sometimes, the stimulus material has to be understood in order to carry out the task. If you have the instruction *Lisez cette lettre et répondez aux questions de votre correspondant*, then you must make sure you find the questions and understand them before you start answering them.

- However, often the stimulus is there to give you a sort of model. This is especially true at Foundation Level, but even at Higher Level you may find useful vocabulary or phrases. For example, a job advertisement will almost certainly contain useful words like *salaire* or *expérience*, and there is no reason not to make use of them in your answer.

- If the tasks are specified by means of questions in French, then you can often at least begin your answer by adapting the question:
  Allez-vous continuer vos études?
  Oui, je vais continuer mes études au lycée, car j'espère aller à l'université.

REVISION SESSION 2 ▬ Different kinds of question ▬ UNIT 17

Each exam board uses different kinds of questions, but there are a number of basic types:

🥖 Foundation Tier _____

- Many boards have as the first question a simple list – single words or short (2–3 word) phrases. This usually carries relatively few marks, and is aimed at Grades F and G. The important thing here is to make sure you only include in the list items which are appropriate to the question. If you're asked to list things to buy for a picnic, don't put down *stylo*.

- The second question is likely to be a message (a postcard/fax/phone message) to be completed in 30–40 words. The tasks (probably five) are clearly specified in French and/or visually, and each will usually require a short sentence. This question is aimed at Grades D, E, F and G. The tasks only require the use of the present tense, in such sentences as: *J'habite une petite maison, J'aime les petits pois; Je joue au volley*

- The third question will probably be a letter to be completed in 70–90 words. The tasks may be set out specifically in French (with or without some sort of French stimulus to help you, such as a letter or an advertisement), or you may simply be asked to reply to a letter which is printed on the question paper. This question is aimed at Grades C and D. The tasks will require the use of past, present and future, (don't forget you can often talk about the future by using *aller* and the infinitive – *Je vais passer les vacances à Paris*) and in addition you will need to give reasons and express opinions.

🥖 Higher Tier _____

- The first question will probably be a letter to be completed in 70–90 words. The tasks may be set out specifically in French (with or without some sort of French stimulus to help you – such as a letter or an advertisement), or you may simply be asked to reply to a letter which is printed on the question paper. (This is in fact the same as the last question on the Foundation paper.) This question is aimed at Grades C and D. The tasks will require the use of past, present and future, (don't forget you can often talk about the future by using *aller* and the infinitive – *Je vais passer les vacances à Paris*) and in addition you will need to give reasons and express opinions.

- The second question will be a letter or an article to be completed in 120-150 words. Again, the tasks may be specified in French, (with or without some sort of French stimulus to help you), or you may be asked to write an account of a series of events outlined in a set of pictures. This question is aimed at Grades A*, A and B. It will often require the use of different tenses, but will also give more scope for a wide range of language, for longer and more detailed descriptions and accounts.

As can be seen on page 127, the Higher Level questions (including the final question on the Foundation paper) may require a number of different forms of writing.

✍ Letters

Whether you are asked to write a formal letter (to a hotel booking a room, or to a company applying for a job, for instance) or an informal letter (to a French-speaking friend), the opening and ending are important.

■ Formal letters usually begin simply *Monsieur, Madame* or *Mademoiselle*. The ending for formal letters is, however, more complex. It is probably enough simply to know one: *Je vous prie d'agréer, Monsieur (Madame, Mademoiselle) l'expression de mes sentiments distingués*. Formal letters require you to use *vous* to the person you are writing to: *Pourriez-vous m'envoyer une liste des hôtels?* It is important to be consistent in this, and to remember to use *votre* and *vos*. Finally, letters will often require you to ask questions. In a formal letter you should use a formal way of asking a question: *Est-ce qu'il y a un musée dans la ville?* or *Y a-t-il un musée dans la ville?*

■ With informal letters, it is normal to begin with *Cher* (*Cher Paul*) or *Chère* (*Chère Marie*). There are several possible endings, varying from the fairly formal *A bientôt* or *Amitiés* to the very familiar *Grosses bises* – only to be used to someone you know well! In informal letters, you will be expected to use *tu* to the person you are writing to. Again, it is important to be consistent, and to use *ton/ta/tes*, and *toi*. Informal letters will usually require you to ask at least one question, but it is quite appropriate to use the colloquial question form, which simply involves the use of a question mark: *Tu as un animal chez toi?*

✍ Articles

■ These are often not very different from letters, apart from the opening and ending referred to above.

■ They are, however, more likely to stick to one subject – where a letter might cover a variety of different topics. It is more important, therefore, (even if the tasks don't ensure this) to make sure that what you write is arranged in some sort of logical order.

■ You are not likely to need to ask questions in an article, so for the sake of variety you might try to use *nous* instead of *je* from time to time: *Je suis allé(e) en France avec mon frère; Nous avons pris le train.*

🥖 Accounts _____

- Accounts are always in the past, but if possible, you should try to get in at least one future. At the end of almost any account, for example, you could put in a sentence like *J'y retournerai l'année prochaine, car je me suis bien amusé(e)*.

- If the account is based on a series of pictures, you don't necessarily need to mention every detail of each picture, but you should make sure that you at least refer to each picture. In fact, when you are making your plan, it is often easier to assume that you will write about the same amount about each picture. So, if you have to write about 150 words based on six pictures, you would expect to write between 20 and 30 words about each picture. This ensures that your account is reasonably balanced.

- These hints, and those which follow, are equally relevant if you are doing the Coursework option.

Higher Level performance

The following tips will all contribute to moving your written work up to and beyond a Grade C. Remember that it is a **requirement** for Grade C that candidates refer to past, present and future events, and express opinions.

■ Each answer should contain references to past, present and future events, and most questions will be designed to encourage use of a variety of tenses. This is not as demanding as it might sound: the perfect tense is easier than the present since there are fewer irregular forms, and the future can usually be expressed by *aller* and the infinitive. It only takes a little imagination to include at least one past and one future in almost any answer. For example, if you have to write about your favourite pop personality, you could simply say where you saw him (*Je l'ai vu à Manchester*) and where he will be playing next (*L'année prochaine, il va chanter à Birmingham*).

■ One of the things which most clearly distinguishes a Grade A/A* piece of work from a Grade C is the length of the sentences produced. It is not difficult to increase the length of your sentences without greatly increasing the complexity of what you write. Simply by using link words such as *mais*, *puis*, *alors* and *donc*, you can combine two sentences into one, and avoid the almost childish impression that a series of short sentences can give. For example:

> *J'ai pris le petit déjeuner, puis je suis parti(e) pour l'école.*
> *Je voudrais une glace, mais je n'ai pas assez d'argent.*

■ Use of *qui* and *que* clauses is another indication of that higher level of language you are looking for, for example:

> *L'homme que j'ai vu était grand et mince.*
> *Chez nous, c'est mon père qui s'occupe du jardin.*

■ Make sure you have some phrases ready for expressing your opinion, for example:

A mon avis	In my opinion
Je pense que/Je crois que	I think that
Il me semble que	It seems to me that

■ Writing at a higher level doesn't just mean writing longer sentences, but writing more fully. Don't just stick to the bare outline.

• Fill in the detail with adjectives:
> *On devait porter un uniforme **rouge** et **jaune***

• Or adverbs:
> ***Soudain** j'ai entendu un bruit.*

• Give explanations:
> *Je me suis couché(e) de bonne heure **car j'étais fatigué(e)***

• Give some background information:
> *Quand je suis arrivé(e), **il pleuvait***

■ Finally, use as wide a variety of language as you can. Just because you've included a perfect tense and a future tense, you don't have to stop at that.

- Try adding an imperfect:
  *Mon père **était** très fâché quand il a vu notre chambre.*

- Or a conditional:
  *Si je gagnais à la loterie, **j'achèterais** une belle moto.*

- And try to avoid repeating words if you can. It isn't always possible, but you can usually manage it with a bit of thought, often by using pronouns. If you've already referred to your case, you can say *Je l'ai laissée dans le train*, and avoid repeating *valise*.

■ *Questions to try* ■

Each examining group sets slightly different styles of questions for the Writing test, as follows:

AQA	**Foundation**	Question 1	A list of 4 items
		Question 2	A message containing 6 sentences
		Question 3	A letter of about 90 words
	Higher	Question 1	As Question 3 above
		Question 2	An article/letter, etc. of about 120 words
Edexcel	**Foundation**	Question 1	A list/questionnaire containing 10 words
		Question 2	Simple phrases
		Question 3	A message containing 30 words
		Question 4	A choice (of letter, etc.) of about 80 words
	Higher	Question 1	As Question 4 above
		Question 2	A choice (of article/letter, etc.) of about 150 words
OCR	**Foundation**	Exercise 1	A list of 8 items
		Exercise 2	Phrases
		Exercise 3	A message of about 40 words
	Higher	Section 1	As Exercise 3 above
		Section 2	A choice (of article/letter, etc.) – about 100 words

The following questions may be different in layout, length, etc. from those set by the different groups, but give useful practice in all the required skills for all groups.

NB The overlap questions (those which appear on **both** Foundation and Higher papers) all require candidates to refer to past, present and future events, and to express personal opinions.

1   You are preparing for a holiday in France. Make a list **in French** of 8 items to take with you.

Exemple _____un short_____

2   What does Hélène do on a Saturday? Fill in the blanks **in French** about Hélène's weekend.

Exemple

Hélène	(SE LEVER)	à	
Hélène	*se lève*	à	*sept heures*

A	Hélène	(PRENDRE)	l'	
	Hélène	——————	l'	——————
B	Hélène	(ALLER)	en	
	Hélène	——————	en	——————
C	Elle	(ACHETER)	une	
	Elle	——————	une	——————
D	Elle	(RENTRER)	à la	
	Elle	——————	à la	——————
E	Elle	(FAIRE)	ses	
	Elle	——————	ses	——————

3 A French boy has sent you an E-mail asking about your family. Give him the following information **in French** in complete sentences:

- how many brothers and sisters you have
- what pets you have
- what **one** member of your family does for a living
- a description of your house
- the personality of **one** member of your family.

Write a letter in reply to Aïcha. Remember to answer all the questions. Write about 70 to 80 words **in French**.

> Paris, le 5 juin
>
> Salut!
>
> C'était comment, tes vacances? Qu'as-tu fait pour t'amuser?
>
> Qu'est-ce que tu vas faire l'année prochaine au collège? Quelles sont tes matières préférées? Que fais-tu le week-end avec tes copains?
>
> Amitiés
>
> **Aïcha**

You have received this letter from your French friend Christophe. He wants to know about your new job. Write about 90 words.

> Salut!
>
> Alors, tu as trouvé un petit job. Où est-ce que tu travailles? Qu'est-ce que tu fais exactement? J'espère que c'est bien payé.
>
> Moi, je n'ai pas de job. Mes parents me donnent de l'argent de poche.
>
> A très bientôt.
>
> Amitiés
>
> Christophe

Ecrivez une lettre à Christophe **en français**. Répondez à ces questions.

- Où travailles-tu?
- Que fais-tu exactement?
- Quelles sont tes heures de travail?
- Tu reçois combien d'argent?
- Qu'est-ce que tu as acheté la semaine dernière avec ton argent?
- Que penses-tu du travail?
- Tu vas faire cette sorte de travail à l'avenir?
- Pourquoi/Pourquoi pas?

6 Vous allez passer deux semaines chez ton ami(e) français(e). Ecrivez une lettre **en français** pour parler de vos passe-temps. Ecrivez 90–100 mots **en français**. Donnez les détails suivants:

- deux activités que vous voudriez faire en France
- ce que vous aimez faire chez vous
- quelque chose que vous n'aimez pas faire
- ce que vous avez fait le week-end dernier.

FOUNDATION + HIGHER

7 Vous avez lu cette lettre dans un magazine.

> J'ai peur pour notre planète. Si on continue comme ça, il n'y aura plus de terre pour nos enfants. Qu'est-ce qu'on peut faire?

HIGHER

Ecrivez une lettre **en français** pour donner vos idées et vos opinions sur les problèmes de l'environnement. Mentionnez:

- les causes de la pollution
- le plus grand problème, à votre avis
- ce que les jeunes peuvent faire
- des autres solutions possibles.

8 Tu écris à ton ami(e) français(e).

> Salut!
>
> Ça va?
>
> Le week-end dernier, je suis allé faire du camping avec mes amis – mais il y a eu un grand problème.
>
> Je vais te dire ce qui s'est passé...

HIGHER

Ecris la lettre jusqu'à la fin (**environ 150 mots**).

9 Vous avez fait un échange en Belgique. Malheureusement, vous ne vous êtes pas très bien amusé(e).

HIGHER

Ecrivez un rapport **en français**. (140–150 mots)

- Parlez de là où votre partenaire habitait (ville/village; maison).
- Donnez vos impressions de sa famille ou de ses ami(e)s.
- Décrivez ce que vous avez fait ensemble.
- Dites si vous allez inviter votre partenaire à venir chez vous. Pourquoi (pas)?

You will find sample answers and examiner's comments on pages 174–9.

UNIT 18: FURTHER GRAMMAR

Most aspects of grammar are covered in the topic units of this book. The chart on pages vi and vii shows you exactly where to find everything. Further grammar not covered elsewhere in the book can be found in this unit.

✍ Possessive pronouns

Singular		Plural		
Masculine	Feminine	Masculine	Feminine	
le mien	*la mienne*	*les miens*	*les miennes*	mine
le tien	*la tienne*	*les tiens*	*les tiennes*	yours
le sien	*la sienne*	*les siens*	*les siennes*	his/hers
le nôtre	*la nôtre*	*les nôtres*	*les nôtres*	ours
le vôtre	*la vôtre*	*les vôtres*	*les vôtres*	yours
le leur	*la leur*	*les leurs*	*les leurs*	theirs

■ Use the appropriate word depending on whether the item is masculine, feminine or plural:

  Marie, j'ai oublié mon stylo.   Marie, I've forgotten my pen.
  Tu me prêtes le tien?   Will you lend me yours?

■ Possession can also be indicated as follows:
  Cette montre est à qui?   Whose is this watch?
  Elle est à moi.   It's mine.

✍ Intensifiers

■ The following indicate how much the quality expressed by an adjective or an adverb is true:

très   very
  Elle était très fâchée.   She was very angry.
  Ils parlent très vite.   They speak very quickly.

trop   too
  Je suis trop fatigué(e).   I'm too tired.
  Le groupe joue trop fort.   The group plays too loudly.

assez   quite
  Il est assez petit.   He's quite small.
  Tu parles assez bien le français.   You speak French quite well.

peu   little
  This is often used instead of *pas très* (not very):
  C'est peu probable.   It's not very likely.

■ The following can be used to indicate how completely the action of a verb is achieved:

tout à fait   completely
  Je n'ai pas tout à fait compris.   I didn't completely understand.

presque   almost/nearly
  Elle a presque fini ses devoirs.   She's nearly finished her homework.

beaucoup   a lot/very much

> *Il me manque beaucoup*   I miss him a lot.

■ These three (as well as *pas beaucoup*, *pas tout à fait* and *un peu*) often stand alone as a one-word answer to a question:

Tu as fini? – Pas tout à fait.	Have you finished? – Not quite.
Vous avez aimé le film?	Did you like the film? – Very
– Beaucoup.	much.
Tu as manqué le car? – Presque.	Did you miss the coach? – Nearly.
Vous parlez français? – Un peu.	Do you speak French? – A little.

Position of pronouns

■ It is sometimes useful to use more than one of these pronouns in a sentence. In this case, there is a fixed order in which they must be used:

1 *je/tu/il/elle/on/nous/vous/ils/elles*
2 *me/te/nous/vous*
3 *le/la/l'/les*
4 *lui/leur*
5 *y*
6 *en*

followed by the verb.

Je voudrais un sandwich.	I'd like a sandwich.
– Il n'y en a plus.	– There aren't any left.
Où est le cadeau de Marie?	Where is Mary's present?
– Je le lui ai déjà donné.	– I've already given it to her.

■ With commands this order changes, in that **2** and **3** change places. Also, *me* becomes *moi* (*m'* before a vowel) and *te* becomes *toi* (*t'* before a vowel). Notice the use of hyphens:

Ça, c'est mon stylo.	That's my pen. Give it to me.
Donnez-le-moi.	
Tu aimes les cerises? Prends-en.	Do you like cherries? Take some.

See also Unit 1.

Relative pronouns

■ *dont*   of which/whom

Voilà le garçon dont je t'ai parlé.	There's the boy I talked to you about (literally: of whom I talked to you).

■ *lequel/laquelle/lesquels/lesquelles*
These are used with prepositions. They must agree with the noun to which they refer:

Voici la boîte dans laquelle	Here's the box in which I found
j'ai trouvé l'argent.	the money.

When used after *à* or *de* these words become:

auquel	*à laquelle*	*auxquels*	*auxquelles*
duquel	*de laquelle*	*desquels*	*desquelles*

> *Lequel*, etc. can also be used as a one-word question:
> | *Voilà la voiture de mon père.* | That's my father's car. |
> | *Laquelle?* | Which one? |

Prepositions

- Some of the more common prepositions cause problems because there is no exact overlap between French and English.

- **about** *au sujet de* (on the subject of)

*Mon père a voulu me parler **au sujet de** mes examens.*	My father wanted to talk to me about my exams.
vers (approximately)	
*Elle est arrivée **vers** neuf heures.*	She arrived about nine o'clock.

- **as far as** *jusqu'à*

  | *Continuez **jusqu'aux** feux rouges.* | Carry on as far as the traffic lights. |

- **before** *avant*

*Elle a mangé **avant** de partir.*	She ate before she left.
déjà (already)	
*J'ai **déjà** vu ce film.*	I've already seen this film./I've seen this film before.

- **by** *à* (means of transport)

à bicyclette/vélo/moto	by bicycle/bike/motorbike
en (means of transport)	
en auto/autobus/avion/bateau/ train/voiture	by car/bus/plane/boat/train/car
par	
*Le président a été tué **par** un assassin.*	The president was killed by an assassin.

- **for** *pendant* (time during which)

*J'ai dormi **pendant** trois heures.*	I slept for three hours.
pour (time in the future)	
*J'irai en France **pour** deux semaines.*	I will go to France for two weeks.
depuis	
*Je la connais **depuis** deux ans.*	I've known her for two years.

- **in** *à* (with names of towns/cities)

à Paris	in Paris
au (with names of masculine countries)	
au Maroc/Portugal/Pays de Galles	in Morocco/Portugal/Wales
aux (with names of countries which are plural)	
aux Antilles/Pays-Bas/Etats-Unis	in the West Indies/Netherlands/ United States
dans (inside)	
*Maman est **dans** le salon.*	Mum is in the living room.
en (with names of most countries)	
en Afrique/Allemagne/Angleterre/ Ecosse/France/Italie	in Africa/Germany/England/ Scotland/France/Italy

- on *à*
  - *à droite/à gauche* on the left/on the right
  - *à pied* on foot
  - *dans* (with means of transport)
  - *Je l'ai vu dans le train.* I saw him on the train.
  - *en*
  - *en vacances* on holiday
  - *sur*
  - *Le livre est sur la table.* The book is on the table.
- since *depuis*
  - *Je suis en Suisse depuis le* I've been in Switzerland since
    onze février. the 11th February.

- until *jusqu'à*
  - *Je serai là jusqu'à huit heures.* I will be there until 8 o'clock.

☜ Conjunctions

- These are linking words, which are useful if you want to create a more complex sentence. Here are some of the most common ones:

alors	so
car	for (because)
donc	so, therefore
et	and
mais	but
ou	or
parce que	because
quand	when

(This is often used with a future tense in French:

Je viendrai te voir quand I'll come and see you when I
  j'aurai le temps. have time.)
si if

(This is followed by either the present or the imperfect tense:

Si je gagne, je t'achèterai If I win I'll buy you a present.
  un cadeau.
Si je gagnais à la loterie, If I won the lottery, I would buy
  j'achèterais une voiture. a car.)

☜ Irregular verbs

The following verbs do not follow the pattern of regular *er*, *ir* or *re* verbs, and you need to learn them individually*:

ALLER – to go
je vais
tu vas
il/elle/on va
nous allons
vous allez
ils/elles vont

APPRENDRE – to learn (see *PRENDRE*)

S'ASSEOIR – to sit down
In the present tense, rarely used except as a command:
Assieds-toi! Sit down!
Asseyez-vous! Sit down!

AVOIR – to have
j'ai
tu as
il/elle/on a
nous avons
vous avez
ils/elles ont

BOIRE – to drink
je bois
tu bois
il/elle/on boit
nous buvons
vous buvez
ils/elles boivent

COMPRENDRE – to understand (see PRENDRE)

CONDUIRE – to drive
je conduis
tu conduis
il/elle/on conduit
nous conduisons
vous conduisez
ils/elles conduisent

CONNAITRE – to know (a person)
je connais
tu connais
il/elle/on connaît
nous connaissons
vous connaissez
ils/elles connaissent

CROIRE – to think/believe
je crois
tu crois
il/elle/on croit
nous croyons
vous croyez
ils/elles croient

COURIR – to run
je cours
tu cours
il/elle/on court
nous courons
vous courez
ils/elles courent

COUVRIR – to cover (see OUVRIR)

DECRIRE – to describe (see ECRIRE)

DEVENIR – to become (see VENIR)

DEVOIR – to have to/should/must
je dois
tu dois
il/elle/on doit
nous devons
vous devez
ils/elles doivent

DIRE – to say
je dis
tu dis
il/elle/on dit
nous disons
vous dites
ils/elles disent

DORMIR – to sleep
je dors
tu dors
il/elle/on dort
nous dormons
vous dormez
ils/elles dorment

ECRIRE – to write
j'écris
tu écris
il/elle/on écrit
nous écrivons
vous écrivez
ils/elles écrivent
(DECRIRE – to describe)

ETRE – to be
je suis
tu es
il/elle/on est
nous sommes
vous êtes
ils/elles sont

FAIRE – to make/do
je fais
tu fais
il/elle/on fait
nous faisons
vous faites
ils/elles font

LIRE – to read
je lis
tu lis
il/elle/on lit
nous lisons
vous lisez
ils/elles lisent

METTRE – to put (on)
je mets
tu mets
il/elle/on met
nous mettons
vous mettez
ils/elles mettent

OFFRIR – to offer (see OUVRIR)

OUVRIR – to open
j'ouvre
tu ouvres
il/elle/on ouvre
nous ouvrons
vous ouvrez
ils/elles ouvrent
(COUVRIR – to cover)
(OFFRIR – to offer)

PARTIR – to leave
je pars
tu pars
il/elle/on part
nous partons
vous partez
ils/elles partent
(SORTIR – to go out)

PLAIRE – to please
Only used in certain phrases:
s'il te/vous plaît   please
Ça (ne) me plaît (pas). I (don't) like it.
Ça te/vous plaît?   Do you like it?

POUVOIR – to be able/can
je peux
tu peux
il/elle/on peut
nous pouvons
vous pouvez
ils/elles peuvent

PRENDRE – to take
je prends
tu prends
il/elle/on prend
nous prenons
vous prenez
ils/elles prennent
(APPRENDRE – to learn)
(COMPRENDRE – to understand)

RECEVOIR – to receive
je reçois
tu reçois
il/elle/on reçoit
nous recevons
vous recevez
ils/elles reçoivent

RIRE – to laugh
je ris
tu ris
il/elle/on rit
nous rions
vous riez
ils/elles rient

SAVOIR – to know (a fact)
je sais
tu sais
il/elle/on sait
nous savons
vous savez
ils/elles savent

SERVIR – to serve
je sers
tu sers
il/elle/on sert
nous servons
vous servez
ils/elles servent

SUIVRE – to follow
je suis
tu suis
il/elle/on suit
nous suivons
vous suivez
ils/elles suivent

SORTIR – to go out (see PARTIR)

TENIR – to hold (see *VENIR*)

VENIR – to come
je viens
tu viens
il/elle/on vient
nous venons
vous venez
ils/elles viennent

(*DEVENIR* – to become)

(*TENIR* – to hold)

VOULOIR – to want (to)
je veux
tu veux
il/elle/on veut
nous voulons
vous voulez
ils/elles veulent

VOIR – to see
je vois
tu vois
il/elle/on voit
nous voyons
vous voyez
ils/elles voient

" Shaded verbs are only
required at Higher Level.

✏ Impersonal verbs

- These are verbs that are only used in the third person singular. The most common examples are probably the weather expressions:

	Present	Imperfect	Perfect	Future
geler – to freeze	*Il gèle*	*Il gelait*	*Il a gelé*	*Il gèlera*
neiger – to snow	*Il neige*	*Il neigeait*	*Il a neigé*	*Il neigera*
pleuvoir – to rain	*Il pleut*	*Il pleuvait*	*Il a plu*	*Il pleuvra*

- The phrase *il y a* (there is/are) is also common:

  *Dans ma chambre, **il y a** un lit et une armoire.* — In my bedroom there is a bed and a wardrobe.

  *Dans mon sac, **il y avait** mes clés.* — In my bag (there) were my keys.

  ***Il y a eu** un embouteillage.* — There was a traffic jam.

  *Demain, **il y aura** du soleil partout.* — Tomorrow there will be sunshine everywhere.

- You also need to be able to recognise *il faut* (it is necessary), though you can usually use *je dois* if you prefer:

  *Dépêche-toi! **Il faut** partir.* — Hurry up! We must leave.

✏ The future perfect tense

- This tense is made up of the future of *avoir* or *être* and the past participle. It is mainly used after:

  quand:
  Quand ils seront arrivés, nous sortirons. — When they arrive, we will go out.

  dès que:
  Dès que j'aurai fini mes examens, je partirai en Italie. — As soon as I have finished my exams, I shall go to Italy.

HIGHER
UNDERSTANDING

The conditional perfect tense

- This tense is often used together with a *si* clause in which the verb is in the pluperfect. It is the equivalent of the English 'If something had happened, I would have ...'

- Its formation is the same as that of the perfect tense, except that the conditional of *avoir* or *être* is used:

    Si je t'avais vu, je t'aurais salué.   If I had seen you, I would have said hello.

    Si j'avais su que tu étais malade,   If I had known you were ill, I
    je serais venu tout de suite.   would have come straight away.

    In the exams set by most boards, this tense will occur only in the Listening and Reading Tests.

The past historic tense

- This tense is not used in speech. It is most often found in literature and journalism, usually in the third person (*il/elle/on/ils/elles*). It will only occur in the Reading Test, and the verb is usually easily recognisable. You should probably not, therefore, spend time learning this unless you are confident that you can cope with everything else on the syllabus.

- There are two types of endings:

er verbs		*ir* and *re* verbs	
je	*-ai*	*je*	*-is*
tu	*-as*	*tu*	*-is*
il/elle/on	*-a*	*il/elle/on*	*-it*
nous	*-âmes*	*nous*	*-îmes*
vous	*-âtes*	*vous*	*-îtes*
ils/elles	*-èrent*	*ils/elles*	*-irent*

- Irregular verbs have the same endings as *ir* and *re* verbs:

je dis	I said
tu fis	you made
il s'assit	he sat down
elle vit	she saw
nous mîmes	we put on
vous prîtes	you took
ils/elles rirent	they laughed

The subjunctive

- This is not a tense, but a form of the verb which is used in certain kinds of structures which use *que*. Like the past historic, it is unlikely to occur except occasionally in the Reading Test, where the verb will be easily recognisable. There are a few irregular verbs where the subjunctive is not so easy to recognise:

aller	→	*j'aille*
avoir	→	*j'aie/il ait*
être	→	*je sois*
faire	→	*je fasse*

HIGHER UNDERSTANDING

List of common verbs

Verbs marked * have minor irregularities – see Unit 2, page 12.

COMMON ER VERBS

accepter	to accept	*brosser*	to brush
accompagner	to go/come with	*se brosser*	to brush
accorder	to grant	*(les dents)*	(one's teeth)
*acheter**	to buy	*cacher*	to hide
adorer	to love	*camper*	to camp
aider	to help	*casser*	to break
aimer	to like	*se casser*	to break
ajouter	to add	*(la jambe)*	(one's leg)
allumer	to light	*cambrioler*	to burgle
améliorer	to improve	*changer*	to change
amuser	to amuse	*chanter*	to sing
s'amuser	to have a	*chercher*	to look for
	good time	*classer*	to sort
annoncer	to announce	*cocher*	to tick
annuler	to cancel	*collectionner*	to collect
*appeler**	to call	*commander*	to order
*s'appeler**	to be called	*commencer**	to begin
apporter	to bring	*composer*	to dial (phone
approuver	to approve (of)		number)
*appuyer**	to lean/to press	*composter*	to stamp
arrêter	to stop	*conseiller*	to advise
	(something else)	*consulter*	to consult
s'arrêter	to stop (oneself)	*conter*	to tell
arriver	to arrive/to	*continuer*	to continue
	happen	*contrôler*	to check
attirer	to attract	*se coucher*	to go to bed
attraper	to catch	*couper*	to cut
augmenter	to add	*coûter*	to cost
avaler	to swallow	*crier*	to shout
se baigner	to bathe	*cultiver*	to grow/to
*balayer**	to sweep		cultivate
bavarder	to chat	*danser*	to dance
blesser	to injure	*débarrasser*	to clear away
bouger	to move	*se débarrasser de*	to get rid of
bricoler	to 'do-it-yourself'	*se débrouiller*	to cope/to get by
briller	to shine	*décider*	to decide
bronzer	to get a sun-tan	*déclarer*	to state

décoller	to take off (aeroplane)	*fumer*	to smoke
		gagner	to win
découper	to cut out	*garer*	to park
décrocher	to lift the receiver (phone)	*geler**	to freeze
		gonfler	to blow up (inflate)
déjeuner	to have lunch		
demander	to ask	*goûter*	to taste
déménager	to move (house)	*habiter*	to live (in)
demeurer	to live	*s'habiller*	to get dressed
dépanner	to repair	*ignorer*	not to know
se dépêcher	to hurry	*imaginer*	to imagine
dépenser	to spend (money)	*indiquer*	to indicate
déposer	to put down	*s'inquiéter**	to worry
déranger	to disturb	*intéresser*	to interest
se déshabiller	to get undressed	*inviter*	to invite
désirer	to want	*jeter**	to throw
dessiner	to draw	*jouer*	to play
se détendre	to relax	*laisser*	to leave
détester	to hate	*laver*	to wash
deviner	to guess	*se lever**	to get up
dîner	to have dinner	*loger*	to stay (accommodation)
discuter	to discuss		
distribuer	to deliver	*louer*	to rent/to hire
donner	to give	*manger**	to eat
doubler	to overtake	*manquer*	to miss
douter	to doubt	(*il me manque* –	I miss him)
durer	to last	*marcher*	to walk/to work (equipment)
écouter	to listen (to)		
écraser	to knock down	*marquer*	to mark
empêcher	to prevent	*mener**	to lead/to take
emporter	to take away	*monter*	to climb/to get on
emprunter	to borrow	*montrer*	to show
enfermer	to shut in	*se moquer de*	to make fun of
*s'ennuyer**	to be bored	*nager*	to swim
enseigner	to teach	*nettoyer**	to clean
entrer	to go/to come in	*noter*	to note down
*envoyer**	to send	*parler*	to speak
*espérer**	to hope	*partager*	to share
*essayer**	to try (on)	*participer*	to take part
*essuyer**	to wipe/to clean	*passer*	to pass
étonner	to surprise	*se passer*	to happen
étudier	to study	*penser*	to think
éviter	to avoid	*persuader*	to persuade
expliquer	to explain	*piquer*	to sting
se fâcher	to get angry	*pleurer*	to cry
féliciter	to congratulate	*plonger*	to dive
fermer	to close	*porter*	to wear/to carry
fêter	to celebrate	*poser*	to put down
freiner	to brake	*poser une question*	to ask a question
frapper	to hit		

pousser	to push/to grow (plants)	*se réveiller*	to wake up	
pratiquer	to practise/to take part in	*rouler*	to travel (car, etc.)	
		saigner	to bleed	
préparer	to prepare	*sauter*	to jump	
présenter	to introduce	*sembler*	to seem	
presser	to squash	*séparer*	to separate	
prêter	to lend	*serrer*	to shake (hands)	
prier	to ask/to beg	*siffler*	to whistle	
*se promener**	to go for a walk	*signer*	to sign	
proposer	to suggest	*soigner*	to take care of	
protester	to protest	*souffler*	to blow	
prouver	to prove	*soulager*	to comfort	
quitter	to leave	*stationner*	to park	
raccommoder	to mend	*supposer*	to suppose	
raccrocher	to hang up (phone)	*taper*	to type	
		téléphoner	to telephone	
raconter	to tell	*se terminer*	to end	
ranger	to tidy	*tirer*	to pull	
se raser	to have a shave	*tomber*	to fall	
recommander	to recommend	*toucher*	to touch	
refuser	to refuse	*tourner*	to turn	
regretter	to regret/ to be sorry	*tousser*	to cough	
		travailler	to work	
		traverser	to cross	
remarquer	to notice	*se tromper*	to make a mistake	
rembourser	to refund			
remercier	to thank	*se tromper (de)*	to get the wrong (number/train)	
rencontrer	to meet			
rentrer	to return	*trouver*	to find	
renverser	to knock over	*se trouver*	to be (situated)	
réparer	to repair	*tuer*	to kill	
*répéter**	to repeat	*utiliser*	to use	
se reposer	to rest	*vérifier*	to check	
réserver	to book/to reserve	*visiter*	to visit	
respirer	to breathe	*voler*	to fly/to steal	
rester	to stay/to remain	*voyager*	to travel	
retourner	to return			

COMMON IR VERBS

choisir	to choose	*réussir*	to succeed
finir	to finish	*saisir*	to grab
remplir	to fill	*vieillir*	to grow old

COMMON RE VERBS

attendre	to wait (for)	*perdre*	to lose
descendre	to go down/ to get off	*rendre*	to give back
		répondre	to answer/to reply
entendre	to hear	*vendre*	to sell

CHECK YOURSELF ANSWERS

UNIT 1: L'ECOLE
1 What you need to know (page 2)

Q1

A Ma matière préférée, c'est les maths.
B Le mercredi, les cours commencent à 9h45.
C Ma sœur est en sixième.
D J'aime le professeur de sciences.
E Il y a beaucoup d'élèves dans mon école.

> **Comments**
>
> **A** Don't forget to put *les* (OR *le/la/l'*) before the subject.
> **B** Remember, you don't need a word for 'on' with days of the week.
> **D** 'The ... teacher' becomes *le professeur de ...* in French.
> **E** *Il y a* is a set phrase which can be singular ('there is') or plural ('there are').

Q2

A l'informatique
B l'allemand
C la biologie
D l'éducation physique
E l'histoire

> **Comments**
>
> **A** You might come across similar words:
> *informaticien*   person who works in IT
> *(bureau) informatisé*   computerised (office).
> **D** It isn't necessarily the subjects which have initials in English (PE, RE, IT) which have initials in French (*l'EPS, l'EMT*).

2 Higher vocabulary (page 4)

Q1

A J'aime les sciences parce que je trouve ça intéressant.
B J'ai choisi l'anglais car le professeur est amusant.
C J'étudie la géographie depuis un an.
D Je ne supporte pas l'histoire à cause des devoirs.
E Je suis nul(le) en musique, malgré le bon professeur.

> **Comments**
>
> **A** If you wrote *J'aime les sciences parce que je les trouve intéressantes*, that is quite correct, but the French often use *ça* in this way, especially to refer to an idea rather than an object.
> **C** Present tense with *depuis*.
> **D** You can only use *parce que* before a verb. You need *des* because *devoirs* is plural.
> **E** Remember that *bon* comes before the noun.

Q2

A Sandrine
B Marc
C Anne

> **Comments**
>
> **A** Thinks school is all right, so it can't be Marc. Hasn't worked, so it can't be Anne.
> **B** All negative comments, but it implies working (*trop de devoirs*) so it can't be Sandrine.
>
> **General** In this sort of item, it isn't just a matter of recognising key words, since none of the people actually says *Je n'aime pas l'école*. You must get the gist, then draw your conclusion.

3 How the grammar works (page 6)

Q1

A le premier août
B à deux heures moins le quart
C de trois heures vingt à quatre heures dix
D Je fais l'allemand depuis cinq ans.
E Regardez (OR Regarde) le tableau!

> **Comments**
>
> **A** The first is different; for other dates just use the numbers 2 to 31.
> **B** The hour comes first, then the minutes.
> **C** from ... to = *de ... à*
> **D** Use the present tense with *depuis*.
> **E** Use *Regardez* if the teacher is talking to the whole class.

Unit 2: A La Maison/ Les Media

1 What you need to know (page 8)

Q1

A passe
B ranges/nettoies
C aidons
D lave
E ai
F fais
G as
H prends

> **Comments**
>
> **A** A singular *er* verb will always end in *–e* except after *tu*.
> **B** After *tu*, any *er* verb will end in *–es*, and all verbs will end in *–s*.
> **C** Apart from *être*, all verbs end in *–ons* after *nous*.
> **E** It is a very common mistake to write (or say) *je* when you mean *j'ai*.
> **F** See **B**.
> **G** See **B**.
> **H** See **B**.

Q2

LA CHAMBRE

A une armoire
B un réveil

LA CUISINE

C le frigo
D un placard
E la cuisinière

LA SALLE DE SEJOUR

F un fauteuil

> **Comments**
>
> You will often need to interpret pictures and other visuals. You have to do this carefully, taking account of all the information you have. You need to make sure that you don't allow one mistake to lead to another. If you are copying words into the right place, make sure you spell them correctly.

2 Higher vocabulary (page 9)

Q1

A Où se trouve la salle de bains?
B Le centre-ville, c'est à quelle distance?
C Je peux téléphoner chez moi?
D Je peux prendre un bains?
E Le déjeuner, c'est à quelle heure?

> **Comments**
>
> **A** When asking where places are, the French will often use *Où se trouve…?* rather than *Où est…?*
> **B** In questions, the French will often use *c'est* or *ce sont* as well as the noun.
> **C** After *je peux* (or any other part of *pouvoir*) the next verb will always be in the infinitive (*er/ir/re*).
> **D** See **C**.
> **E** See **B**.

Q2

Best order: **C – A – E – B – D**

Full account:

Le matin, je me lève à sept heures et demie et je me lave <u>dans la salle de bains</u>. Puis je m'habille <u>dans ma chambre</u>, <u>et</u> je prends <u>mon</u> petit déjeuner <u>dans la cuisine</u>. <u>A huit heures et demie</u> je vais à l'école.

> **Comments**
>
> The addition of the underlined items, especially in the Speaking Test, will improve your marks by turning a series of brief answers into a full, though still simple, account.

3 How the grammar works (page 12)

Q1

A J'écoute la radio.
B Je me lave dans la salle de bains.
C Il finit ses devoirs.
D Tu veux (*OR* Vous voulez) sortir?
E Je ne comprends pas.

> **Comments**
>
> **A** 'I listen to'/'I am listening to' are the same in French.
> **B** Don't forget the reflexive pronoun.
> **C** See **A**.
> **D** You could say *Veux-tu* or *Est-ce que tu veux* here.
> **E** *Comprendre* is just like *prendre*.

Unit 3: La Sante, La Forme et La Nourriture

1 What you need to know (page 14)

Q1

A J'ai mal au genou.

B J'ai mal à l'oreille.

C Je suis enrhumé(e).

D J'ai mal aux yeux.

E Je me suis cassé la jambe.

> **Comments**
>
> A Use *au* because *genou* is masculine.
>
> B Remember *l'* before a vowel.
>
> C Symptoms are not always expressed by *avoir mal*. You need the correct part of *être* here – and remember, if you are female, to add an *-e* to *enrhumé*.
>
> D Did you remember the unusual plural of *œil*?
>
> E Because of the reflexive pronoun *me*, don't use the possessive *ma* in front of *jambe*.

Q2

A Je n'ai pas de couteau.

B Je n'aime pas vraiment le poulet.

C Je n'ai pas faim.

D J'ai besoin d'une aspirine.

E Tu me passes une cuillère, s'il te plaît?

> **Comments**
>
> A Remember to use *de* after *ne ... pas*.
>
> B Don't forget that you need to include the definite article (*le*) here.
>
> D *J'ai besoin* is always followed by *de*.
>
> E Use *tu* (and therefore *s'il te plaît*) to your penfriend. To his/her mother you would say *Vous me passez une cuillère, s'il vous plaît?*

2 Higher vocabulary (page 15)

Q1

A Ma truite n'est pas assez cuite.

B Le service était très lent.

C Mon café est froid.

D Il y a une erreur dans l'addition.

E Les frites sont brûlées.

> **Comments**
>
> A *Truite* is feminine, so *ma* and *cuite* must agree.
>
> B Remember to use a past tense.
>
> C *Café* is masculine, so use *mon*.
>
> D When you check a word in the dictionary, make sure you check its gender.
>
> E *Frites* is feminine plural, so *brûlées* must agree.

Q2

A au

B de

C des

D de la

E à la

> **Comments**
>
> A It's *le cinema*, and *à* + *le* = *au*.
>
> B After a negative, *des* becomes *de*.
>
> C 'Some' (plural) = *des*.
>
> D *Confiture* is feminine.
>
> E To describe a flavour or a filling, use *à*:
>
> | | |
> |---|---|
> | (glace) *à la menthe* | mint (ice cream) |
> | (tarte) *aux fraises* | strawberry (tart) |
> | (saucisson) *à l'ail* | garlic (sausage) |

3 How the grammar works (page 18)

Q1

A trois chevaux

B des couteaux

C Je n'ai pas de cuillère.

D J'adore le jambon.

E Je mange le chocolat en regardant la télévision.

> **Comments**
>
> A Nouns ending in ...*al* (like *cheval*) make their plural in ...*aux*.
>
> B 'Some', with a plural, is *des*.
>
> C Use *de* (not *de la*) after a negative.
>
> D Use the definite article (*le*) because it refers to ham in general.
>
> E *En* with the present participle indicates simultaneous actions.

Unit 4: Moi, Ma Famille et Mes Amies

1 What you need to know (page 20)

Q1

A Ma tante habite chez nous.

B Il est né le 23 septembre.

C Elle porte des lunettes.

D Je m'entends bien avec mes parents.

E Elle a les cheveux gris.

> **Comments**
>
> A Use *ma* because *tante* is female.
>
> B You don't need to write out numbers, but you do need to know them!
>
> D Use *mes* because *parents* is plural.
>
> E Don't add –s to *gris*; it already has one.

Q2

A My sister is 15.

B She is not married.

C His name is Louis.

D My grandfather is 80.

> **Comments**
>
> A Numbers are very easy to confuse, especially in listening:
> *cinq* (5) and *quinze* (15)
> *quatre-vingts* (80) and *vingt-quatre* (24).
>
> B Make sure you don't miss negatives. Again, this is especially easy to do in listening.
>
> C Pronouns are very important:
> *je* (I); *il* (he); *elle* (she).
>
> D See **A**.

2 Higher vocabulary (page 21)

Q1

A Nous n'aimons pas la même musique.

B Je ne peux pas rentrer après dix heures et demie.

C Je m'entends assez bien avec mon père, mais je ne peux pas vraiment lui parler.

D Ma belle-mère est plus âgée que mon père.

E Tu t'entends bien avec tes frères et sœurs?

F Ma meilleure amie s'appelle Marie. Elle a dix-sept ans, et elle habite avec son père. Ses parents sont divorcés.

> **Comments**
>
> A The adjective *même* doesn't change in the singular.
>
> B Note: *il peut* but *je peux*.
>
> C Little words like *assez* and *vraiment* can really improve your work.
>
> D *Agée* goes with *belle-mère*. Remember, when you are comparing, put *plus* (or *mois* – less, or *aussi* – as) in front of the adjective, and *que* after it.
>
> F Did you get the adjectives right? *Ma meilleure amie; son père; ses parents divorcés.*

Q2

A ✗

B ✓

C ✓

D ✓

E ✗

> **Comments**
>
> A Even if you didn't understand the rest, *ce n'est pas juste* gives you the answer.
>
> B Use any clues you can: you may never have seen *gâtent*, but look in **Higher vocabulary** and find *gâté*.
>
> C Watch for negatives when people are expressing opinions, but be careful. *Il n'y a jamais de disputes* isn't really a negative thing to say.
>
> D Opinions aren't always black or white – people sometimes express both sides of the argument, and you have to draw a conclusion. Are the disputes more important than the *meilleure amie*?
>
> E Again, you will often hear things which are not relevant to the question – you have to sort it out.

3 How the grammar works (page 22)

Q1

A une petite maison

B Ma mère est plus grande que moi.

C Elle est italienne.

D Il a les cheveux marron.

E Ma sœur est gentille.

Comments

A *Maison* is feminine, and *petite* comes before the noun.

B The adjective agrees with *mère*, and is feminine.

C Note the irregular feminine.

D *Marron* does not change to agree with the noun.

E Note the irregular feminine.

UNIT 5: LE TEMPS LIBRE, LES LOISIRS, LES VACANCES ET LES FÊTES

1 What you need to know (page 24)

Q1

A faux
B vrai
C vrai
D faux
E faux

Comments

A You need to spot the word *seulement* (only) to get this right.

B 3 for price of 2 = 6€.

C 50% off for a group of 10.

D Students only get 30% off (they actually pay 2.19€).

E You have to be under 15 to pay only 1€.

Q2

A 3
B 4
C 1
D 5
E 2

2 Higher vocabulary (page 25)

Q1

A 4
B 7
C 1
D 10
E 3

Comments

A *Devoir* is followed simply by the infinitive.

B *Commencer* takes *à* before the infinitive – and remember, 'to be cold' is *avoir froid*.

C *Essayer* takes *de* before the infinitive.

D *Décider* takes *de* before the infinitive – and remember, you need to use the right reflexive pronoun, even with the infinitive, in this case *te*.

E If the verb uses *être* for the perfect tense, the past participle must agree (*arrivée*).

Q2

A Le week-end dernier, je suis allé(e) à Paris.

B Mon grand-père m'a donné huit euros.

C Je dois faire le ménage pour gagner de l'argent.

D J'aime regarder la télévision.

E Oui, je suis d'accord avec toi.

Comments

A *Aller* is one of the verbs which uses *être*. Remember to add an extra *-e* if you are female.

B The pronoun *me* loses its *e* before a vowel.

C Two infinitives here: the first after *devoir*, the second after *pour* ('in order to').

D *Aimer* is followed simply by the infinitive.

E To agree = *être d'accord*.

3 How the grammar works (page 28)

Q1

A Je vais écouter la radio.

B Nous avons fait la vaisselle.

C Il a commencé à faire ses devoirs.

D Ils sont allés (*OR* Elles sont allées) au cinéma.

E Elle est rentrée à dix heures.

Comments

A *Aller* is followed directly by the infinitive.

B Note the irregular past participle.

C *Commencer* has *à* before the infinitive.

D Note the agreement of the past participle (because *aller* takes *être*).

E See **D**.

Unit 6: Les Rapports Personnels, Les Activites Sociales et Les Rendez-vous

1 What you need to know (page 30)

Q1

A Je n'aime pas les films policiers.

B Je dois faire le ménage.

C On se rencontre devant le cinéma?

D On se voit à dix-neuf heures trente/sept heures et demie?

E Tu veux venir au match de foot samedi?

Comments

A Remember to make *policiers* plural, to agree with *films*.

B *Devoir* is followed immediately by the infinitive.

C 'Outside' a place is usually expressed by *devant*.

D You can either use the 24-hour clock or the 12-hour clock, but be consistent. The 24-hour clock is always just a number of hours followed by a number of minutes. It never uses expressions like 'half past'.

E *Vouloir* is followed immediately by the infinitive.

Q2

A Je veux bien, merci./D'accord.

B Qu'est-ce qu'il y a comme film?

C La séance commence à quelle heure?

D Où est-ce qu'on se rencontre?

E Je dois rentrer avant minuit.

Comments

A *D'accord* shows a little less enthusiasm.

B This expression using *comme* is very useful for finding out what sort of thing is available, as also in *Qu'est-ce que tu aimes comme films?*

C It's best to find out what time the programme (*la séance*) begins.

D *On* is very often used instead of *nous* in everyday conversation.

E *Rentrer* often means 'to return' in the sense of 'to go home'.

2 Higher vocabulary (page 31)

Q1

A Je ne les aime pas.

B Il y va demain.

C Elle lui a écrit hier.

D J'en ai trois.

E Pierre les a mangées.

Comments

A Remember to use *les* (or *le/la*) for generalisations.

B You need the word *y* even though there's no word in English.

C Use *lui* for 'to him' or 'to her'.

D You need *en* even though there's no word in English.

E Add –*es* to the past participle, because *cerises* are feminine plural.

Q2

A Non, je ne peux pas. Je vais chez Isabelle.

B Non, je ne peux pas. Je vais en ville pour faire des courses.

C Non, je regrette. Mercredi je vais au cinéma.

D Je m'excuse. Je l'ai déjà vu.

E Oui, je veux bien. J'adore le foot.

Comments

A-D It doesn't matter which of the forms of apology you use, but make it polite!

B Remember *pour* with the infinitive – 'in order to'.

C No need for a word for 'on' with days of the week.

D Remember that the object pronoun comes before *avoir* in the perfect tense.

E When accepting an invitation, sound enthusiastic!

3 How the grammar works (page 34)

Q1

A Je l'ai vue hier.

B Je vous (OR t') ai écrit une lettre.

C la fille qui mange une glace

D le garçon que j'ai vu en ville

E Je vais avec toi (OR vous).

Comments

A Note that the pronoun (*l'*) comes before *ai*. Note also the agreement of the past participle (because *l'* refers to a girl).

B See **A** (first part).

C *Qui* refers to the subject of the verb.

D *Que* refers to the object of the verb.

E Use *moi, toi,* etc. after a preposition.

UNIT 7: LA VILLE, LES REGIONS ET LE TEMPS
1 What you need to know (page 36)

Q1

A Dans l'est

B il pleuvra

C dans l'ouest

D la température maximale sera de vingt-trois degrés

E dans le nord-est

Comments

A To understand weather forecasts, the region can be as important as the weather itself.

B In forecasts, the normal tense is the future.

C See **A**.

D Numbers can be important in weather forecasts.

E The points of the compass combine in French just as they do in English.

Q2

A town

B country

C country

D town

E country

Comments

A Words like *beaucoup* can reveal a lot about attitudes.

B *Trop* reveals the attitude, but you need the second sentence to make it clear that the speaker doesn't live in the town.

C Here, you need to understand the gist. There is no specific word which gives you the answer.

D See **C**.

E The negative makes all the difference.

2 Higher vocabulary (page 37)

Q1

A Demain, j'irai en ville.

B Nous prendrons le dîner à sept heures.

C Tu regarderas la télé ce soir?

D Ils achèteront des CDs.

E Samedi elle aura dix-sept ans.

Comments

A *Aller* is irregular in the future.

B *Prendre* is more common than both *avoir* and *manger* when talking about meals.

D *Acheter* is slightly irregular (*achèteront*).

E Remember: age is expressed by using *avoir* – and you always include *ans*.

Q2

A La voile est plus passionnante que le tennis.

B Paul est plus âgé que son frère.

C Les filles sont aussi intelligentes que les garçons.

D Les cheveux d'Anne sont plus courts que les cheveux de Marie.

E Les films d'amour sont moins amusants que les westerns.

Comments

This sort of activity, building up an account from notes, is used by exam boards. Also, making notes like this in preparation for a written question is much more useful than doing the answer in rough and then writing it out in neat. It gives you a pattern for sentences, and will help you to avoid the common error of thinking a sentence out in English and then translating it into French. That would almost certainly result in producing sentences with grammatical mistakes, and which don't read like French.

A *Passionnante* agrees with *voile*.

C *Intelligentes* agrees with *les filles*.

D Remember: *cheveux* is plural, so *courts* must agree.

E Again, *amusants* agrees with *les films*.

3 How the grammar works (page 39)

Q1

A Claire est moins grande que Marie.

B Elle fera le lit.

C Ils (*OR* Elles) viendront demain.

D Tu seras à la maison (*OR* chez toi)? *OR* Vous serez à la maison (*OR* chez vous)?

E Je préférerais une pomme.

> **Comments**
>
> **A** You could say ...*n'est pas aussi grande que*..., but it's more clumsy.
>
> **B** Note the irregular future of *faire*.
>
> **C** See **B**.
>
> **D** See **B**.
>
> **E** Use the conditional to express '...would'.

UNIT 8: LES COURSES ET LES SERVICES PUBLICS

1 What you need to know (page 41)

Q1

A Je voudrais une veste grise, s'il vous plaît.

B Elle est trop petite.

C Vous avez la même chose en plus grand?

D C'est combien?

E Je la prends.

> **Comments**
>
> **A** Of course, there are other ways of asking for things in shops: *Avez-vous...?/Donnez-moi...*
>
> **B** *Elle* and *petite* because *veste* is feminine.
>
> **E** *La* because *veste* is feminine.

Q2

A 4

B 1

C 2

D 5

E 3

> **Comments**
>
> This sort of exercise, which you might find in the Reading Test, is one which depends entirely on understanding individual words. It is therefore an ideal example of where you can most effectively use techniques such as looking for similarities with English words.

2 Higher vocabulary (page 42)

Q1

A J'ai acheté cette radio hier. Elle ne marche pas.

B J'ai acheté ce chemisier samedi. Il est déchiré.

C Ma mère m'a acheté ce pull. Il est beaucoup trop grand.

> **Comments**
>
> **A/B** Remember to use *il* or *elle* according to the gender of the noun being referred to.
>
> **B** Remember there is no word for 'on' with days of the week.
>
> **C** *Me* (here *m'*) in front of the verb can often mean 'for me'. Remember to give all the details – don't leave out *beaucoup*.

Q2

A J'ai laissé ma veste dans le train.

B Elle est bleue, en coton.

C Dans la poche, il y avait un billet de vingt euros...

D ... et une montre en or.

> **Comments**
>
> **A** With public transport, the French say *dans* for 'on'.
>
> **B** When saying what something is made of, always put *en* in front of the material. The material is a noun, so don't add *–e*, even if the item is feminine.
>
> **C** A 20€ note is *un billet de vingt euros* (but a 0,46€ stamp is *un timbre à zéro virgule quarante-six euros*).
>
> **D** See **B**.

3 How the grammar works (page 45)

Q1

A soixante-dix-sept

B quatre-vingt-quinze

C douzième

D deux cent cinquante grammes de pêches

E un verre de vin

Comments

A Numbers in the seventies and nineties require careful thought.

B See **A**.

C Note the omission of the final *e* from *douze*.

D Numbers combine in very much the same way as in English.

E A quantity (such as *verre*) is always followed by *de*.

UNIT 9: LA ROUTE, LES VOYAGES ET LES TRANSPORTS

1 What you need to know (page 47)

Q1

A Au carrefour, tournez à droite.

B Aux feux, continuez tout droit.

C Après l'église, prenez la troisième à gauche.

D Continuez jusqu'au rond-point, et tournez à droite.

Comments

A Don't confuse *droit* (straight on) and *droite* (right).

B In *droite* the final −*t* is pronounced; in *droit* it is silent.

C Landmarks like churches are often used in directions. Here, you need *après*: it wouldn't make sense to say *à l'église*.

D You often link two separate instructions with *et*.

Q2

A Je voudrais un aller simple pour Dieppe, s'il vous plaît.

B Je voudrais un aller-retour, première classe, pour Dijon, s'il vous plaît.

C A quelle heure part le train?

D Il y a un train pour Le Havre cet après-midi?

Comments

A/B In role-plays, you are often expected to ask a question, and to do so politely. You may lose marks if you don't. It is also important to get in all the information you are given.

C Apart from *C'est combien?* ('How much is it?'), *A quelle heure?* is one of the most likely questions you will be asked to produce.

D You often need to combine language from different topics to carry out a task. Here, *cet après-midi* has not been covered specifically within this unit.

2 Higher vocabulary (page 49)

Q1

A Je suis allé(e) à l'aéroport en car.

B L'avion est parti à dix-huit heures dix-huit.

C Je suis arrivé à vingt heures trente.

D J'ai pris un taxi pour aller à l'hôtel.

E C'était à vingt minutes de l'aéroport.

Comments

If you are asked to describe an event in the past, make sure you use the appropriate tenses (see Unit 12).

B Remember the use of the 24-hour clock in timetables. The prompts would probably lead you to begin both sentences with *L'avion*, but it is always a good idea to introduce variety when you can.

C See **B**.

D If you say *J'ai pris un taxi à l'hôtel* it means you got in the taxi at the hotel. You need to add *pour aller* to make your meaning clear.

Q2

A bateau

B tunnel sous la Manche

C train

D vélo

E car

Comments

Don't be tempted to jump in too quickly; you may need the gist of the whole utterance before you can answer. There is sometimes a key phrase, such as *voyager sous la mer* in **B**, but sometimes you may simply have to put all the information together.

A The key here is *ce n'est pas très rapide*.

C It's really *assez* that tells you this isn't about the plane.

D Perhaps the real clue here is *C'est fatigant*.

E Here it really is a question of putting the whole thing together.

3 How the grammar works (page 52)

Q1

A As-tu (*OR* Avez-vous) aimé le film?

B Tu regardes (*OR* Vous regardez) souvent la télévision?

C Qu'est-ce que tu regardes (*OR* vous regardez)?

D Où vas-tu (*OR* allez-vous)?

E A quelle heure est-ce que tu manges (*OR* vous mangez)?

Comments

A Remember there are different ways of asking **Check yourself questions**. Use the one which comes easiest to you.

B If you are writing this question, you must put in the question mark.

C Do not invert the verb after (*Qu'*)*est-ce que*.

D After question words (like *où*) it is most common to invert the verb.

E Don't forget the *à* when asking what time something happens.

UNIT 10: L'ENSEIGNEMENT SUPERIEUR, LA FORMATION ET L'EMPLOI
1 What you need to know (page 54)

Q1

A Je travaille au supermarché.

B Je travaille de dix-sept heures à dix-neuf heures du lundi au vendredi.

C Je gagne vingt-cinq livres par semaine.

D Je n'aime pas le travail.

E Je fais des économies pour acheter des vêtements.

Comments

A Your exam board will have a set of icons like these to represent common objects and ideas. You should make sure you are familiar with them.

B Make sure you give both bits of information – failure to do so could well cost you more than half marks.

C Here, *par semaine* is again an important part of the message, which you mustn't leave out.

D There are lots of other things you could say here. *C'est ennuyeux/fatigant/mal payé* would fit equally well.

E If you couldn't remember *faire des économies*, you could say instead *J'achète des vêtements avec l'argent*, which would be almost as good.

Q2

A travaille dans un bureau

B est caissier

C est facteur

D est fermier

E travaille au syndicat d'initiative

Comments

This sort of question is often a matter of vocabulary. If you are really stuck for a word, there are some things you can do before you resort to sheer guesswork!

A You may have forgotten *ordinateur*, but there are plenty of other words which give you the answer.

B There are lots of clues to help here. Who else in the list might deal with money?

C If you don't know *courrier*, look at the list of jobs. Is there one who gets up early to deliver something?

D There's only one of these jobs that could involve animals.

E If you really can't remember *syndicat d'initiative*, with any luck, this is the only one left anyway!

2 Higher vocabulary (page 56)

Q1

A professeur de gymnastique
B réceptionniste dans un cabinet de médecin
C mécanicien
D chauffeur de camion
E coiffeuse

Comments

A The mention of *adolescents* rules out *moniteur de ski*.
B You need to understand the first half of the sentence to eliminate *médecin*.
C Here, what is said about school is not really relevant, because it is outweighed by *ce que j'aime le mieux*.
D *Voyager* is the real clue, though you could have been misled by *voiture* in **C**.
E You need to understand the gist, and then draw a conclusion.

Q2

A 3
B 4
C 1
D 5
E 2

Comments

For this exercise, you really need quite a detailed understanding of both the vocabulary and the structures to work out the answers.

A The specific languages should make the link with *langues* (and not with *Belgique* – they are the wrong languages!).
B In this sort of exercise, you need to keep an eye on the whole exercise. If you choose 2 as your answer here (it's just about logical), you are left with nothing for **E**.
C This is the only beginning which can be followed without a linking word, as it's already there in *avant de*.
D A sentence with an imperfect tense can easily be followed by a contrast (*mais*).
E The conditional tense is important here ('Why would one work').

3 How the grammar works (page 58)

Q1

A Nous n'allons jamais au cinéma.
B Il n'y a plus de gâteau.
C Elle n'a qu'un frère.
D Je n'ai rien vu.

Comments

A The *ne* and the other part of the negative go round the verb in the present.
B See **A**.
C See **A**.
D In the past, the *ne* and the other part of the negative go round the part of *avoir* or *être*.

UNIT 11: LA PUBLICITE, LES COMMUNICATIONS ET LES LANGUES AU TRAVAIL
1 What you need to know (page 60)

Q1

A un yaourt
B un shampooing
C un magasin de disques
D un magazine pour les jeunes
E un pull

Comments

A You always need to be careful with the first answer in this sort of question. It's true that *yaourt* might fit, but is there anything else which might fit better? Here there isn't!
B Be careful not to answer on the basis of just one word. For example, *santé* could be appropriate for yogurt. It's only when you get to *cheveux* that you have enough information.
C Don't confuse *magazine* and *magasin* (shop).
D Try to be aware of French words which look like English words. There are a lot of them, and it can save you time.
E *Coton* might have made you think about *une machine à laver*, but the *en* should give you the correct answer.

Q2

A plus tard
B Téléphonez
C rendez-vous
D en retard
E bureau

Comments

A The difference between *plus tard* (later) and *en retard* (late) is crucial in these.

B *Rendez-vous* would only fit here if the next word was *avec*, not *à*.

C *Téléphoné* would fit here, but not *téléphonez*, so the only possibility is *rendez-vous*.

D See **A**.

E Again, *téléphone* would fit, but not *téléphonez*.

2 Higher vocabulary (page 62)

Q1

A Je suis libre aux mois de juillet et août.
B J'ai déjà travaillé dans un restaurant.
C Je m'entends bien avec les clients.
D Je voudrais travailler le soir, mais pas le week-end.
E Je gagnerai combien?

Comments

A 'In' with a month is *en* (not *dans*), but *au mois de* is also very common. Here, *aux* has to be plural since it refers to both July and August.

B In the past, *déjà* comes before the past participle.

C You need to be able to create new sentences by substituting fresh elements: you know *je m'entends bien avec*, and you can add all sorts of new endings.

D Remember this use of *pas* without *ne*.

E There is often another way of expressing an idea, if you're not sure of a word. For example, here you could say: *Le salaire, c'est combien?* or even *Ça paie combien?*

Q2

A Je dois répondre au téléphone – c'est difficile en français.
B Je dois aider les clients anglais.
C Je m'entends très bien avec le directeur.
D Je dois travailler un week-end sur deux, mais je suis libre le vendredi and le lundi.
E Le salaire n'est pas énorme, mais ce n'est pas mal.

Comments

A To answer the phone = *répondre au téléphone*.

A/B Remember: *devoir* is followed by the infinitive.

C Don't leave out the little words – *très* is an important part of the message.

D 'Every other' is easily expressed in French by *un ... sur deux*. In the same way, *un ... sur trois/quatre* means 'one in three/four'.

E You could use *formidable* (great) here, but when referring to size, and particularly money, the French often use *enorme*. *Ce ne n'est pas* (or *C'est pas*) *mal* is very commonly used for 'It's not bad'.

3 How the grammar works (page 64)

Q1

A C'est le garçon le plus intelligent du collège.
B C'est la publicité la plus amusante.
C Je n'aime pas ce professeur.
D J'adore cette émission.

Comments

A After a superlative, 'in the' is *du* (or *de la* or *des*)

B Don't forget to make the definite article and the adjective agree (*la plus amusante*).

C If the teacher is a woman, you would say *cette professeur*.

D Note the unusual feminine form of the adjective.

Unit 12: La Vie A L'etranger, Le Tourisme, Les Coutumes et Le Logement

1 What you need to know (page 66)

Q1

A Je voudrais une chambre pour deux personnes, avec salle de bains.

B Avez-vous une chambre pour une personne pour un nuit?

C Je voudrais une chambre pour une personne avec douche et WC.

D Il y a une télévision dans la chambre?

E A quelle heure est le petit déjeuner?

Comments

A Your exam board will use icons of this sort to represent various kinds of room. Make sure you can recognise them easily.

B The question mark tells you to ask a question.

C Make sure you give all the required details.

D The phrase *il y a* is very useful when you want to find out if something is available. In speech, don't forget to use a rising tone to make it a question.

E Finding out what time something is, is one of the most likely questions you will need to ask. Make sure you can do it.

Q2

A emplacement

B après

C fermée

D avant

E dortoir

Comments

A After *un*, there must be a noun. There are four nouns in the list, but do you really want a restaurant, a garage or a dormitory for your tent and caravan? *Emplacement* is a hard word to translate, but it just means the bit of land (pitch) on which you put your tent.

B *Avant* (before) would fit here grammatically, but logically it makes no sense.

C Again, *ouverte* would fit grammatically, but not logically.

D As in **B**, you need to use your common sense as well as your knowledge of French.

E The youth hostel is not likely to have a restaurant *especially* for girls, so the answer must be *dortoir*.

2 Higher vocabulary (page 68)

Q1

A Je voudrais réserver une chambre pour deux semaines …

B … du vingt-trois juillet au cinq août.

C Je voudrais une chambre pour deux personnes, avec douche et WC, en demi-pension.

D Pourriez-vous m'envoyer des brochures sur la région?

E Pourriez-vous me confirmer ma réservation?

Comments

A *Quinze jours* is more common than *deux semaines* to mean 'a fortnight'.

B Remember *du* and *au* with dates: 'from … to'.

C Instead of *en demi-pension* you could equally correctly say *avec petit déjeuner et dîner*.

D/E *Pourriez-vous* is a very polite way of asking someone to do something for you, the equivalent of 'Could you' or 'Would you' in English.

E It probably wouldn't matter if you said *la* réservation instead of **ma**.

Q2

A Annie

B Samir

C Maryse

D Chloé

E Rachelle

Comments

A You have to deduce that the traffic noise kept her awake, so that she came home tired.

B In the first 1¹⁄₂ sentences, you can work out that he is being complimentary about the hotel, even if you don't understand *impeccable* ('faultless'). However, to understand the 'but', you probably need to look up *animé* ('lively'), as that is the link with 'bored'.

C *Malgré* means 'in spite of', so you are clearly looking for someone who had a poor hotel, but still had a good time.

D This is hard – everything she says about the holiday is good except that she was bored.

E You have to deduce that, since she has already booked again, she had a really good time.

3 How the grammar works (page 70)

Q1

A Nous finissions nos devoirs.
B Elle mangeait beaucoup.
C Tu étais (*OR* Vous étiez) déjà sorti(e).
D Le camping était près de la plage.
E J'ai vu le film quand j'étais à Paris.

Comments

A Be careful when writing the *nous* form of the imperfect: it's easy to miss out the *i* in *finissions*.

B Use the imperfect for 'used to'.

C Use the pluperfect for 'had ...'.

D Use the imperfect for description in the past.

E Here you use the perfect for the completed action, and the imperfect for the description.

UNIT 13: LE MONDE
1 What you need to know (page 72)

Q1

A Je suis allé(e) aux Pays-Bas l'année dernière.
B La ville la plus importante est Amsterdam.
C Tous les Hollandais parlent anglais.
D L'année prochaine j'irai en Afrique.
E Je voudrais faire le tour du monde.

Comments

A If you are female, make *allée* agree. Remember that *Pays-Bas* is masculine plural, so use *aux*.

B To say 'the most...', you have to repeat the definite article (*la ... la plus ...*).

C When referring to the people of a country, use a capital letter (but not when it's an adjective, or a language).

D To or in with continents is *en*.

E *Je voudrais* can be used for saying what you'd like to do, as well as asking for something (*Je voudrais un café*). Notice *faire le tour de* = to go round.

Q2

A C'est la Suisse.
B C'est l'Espagne.
C C'est l'Ecosse.
D C'est la Belgique.
E C'est l'Allemagne.

Comments

A Note that the capital of Switzerland is not *Genève*, as many people think.

B The combined compass points – *nord-est*, *sud-ouest*, etc. can be easy to miss.

C Names of cities are almost always the same in French as in English – except for *Londres*, *Edimbourg* and *Douvres* (Dover).

D Unlike in Switzerland, where many people speak at least two of the official languages, in Belgium most people speak either one or the other, not both.

E In French, East Germany used to be referred to as *la RDA* and West Germany as *la RFA*.

2 Higher vocabulary (page 74)

Q1

A énergie
B pétrole
C conserver
D voiture
E bouteilles

Comments

A An easy one to start: it's the only word which begins with a vowel.
B *Bouteilles, vent* and *papier* would also fit grammatically, but none makes sense.
C After *essayer de*, the next word must be an infinitive.
D This is the only answer which fits with *vélo*.
E It could be *papier*, except that *toutes* is feminine plural.

Q2

A la sécheresse
B la faim
C les espèces en danger
D la pollution de l'atmosphère
E la pollution des eaux

Comments

A *Pluie* could link with *pollution des eaux* or *pluie acide* but this is clearly about drought.
B *Trop de personnes* might lead you to *surpopulation*, but the gist obviously refers to lack of food.
C Put *tuer* and *disparaître* together and this is the only possible answer.
D You have to understand the whole sentence to pick out the right answer here. There is no word-to-word link.
E The connection between *rivières, plages* and *eaux* should be fairly clear.

3 How the grammar works (page 76)

Q1

A Où sont les autres?
B As-tu (*OR* Avez-vous) perdu quelque chose?
C Tout le monde est heureux.
D Il a battu tous les records.

Comments

A *Autres* can be used as a noun.
B *Quelque chose* is two separate words, unlike *quelquefois* (sometimes).
C The verb with *tout le monde* is always singular.
D Note the irregular masculine plural of *tout*.

Unit 14: Exam practice
Listening and responding (pages 90–1)

Transcripts

 1 Vous pouvez dîner entre sept heures et demie et neuf heures.

2 Avant de quitter l'hôtel, voulez-vous rendre la clé à la réception, s'il vous plaît?

3 Dans le nord, il y aura de la pluie un peu partout.

Dans l'ouest, la température maximale sera de treize degrés.

Dans l'est, il fera un temps ensoleillé.

Dans le sud, le vent soufflera jusqu'à quarante kilomètres-heure.

4 Moi, j'aime les vacances actives, tu sais, et puis j'habite pas loin des Alpes, alors je prends plutôt mes vacances l'hiver. Je n'aime pas trop voyager.

5 Ce soir à vingt et une heures trente sur la place du marché, grand cirque russe. Achetez vos billets jusqu'à quinze heures au syndicat d'initiative – adultes neuf euros cinquante, enfants six euros – ou à l'entrée – adultes onze euros cinquante, enfants sept euros cinquante. Nous vous informons qu'aucun animal sauvage ne fait partie de ce cirque.

6 Allô. Est-ce que je peux laisser un message pour Mme Lucas, s'il vous plaît? Ici M. Dupond – D U P O N D. Pouvez-vous lui dire que je l'attendrai à l'office du tourisme à seize heures quinze? Merci.

7 – Tous les ans, on va au bord de la mer. J'adore les sports nautiques.
– Mais Jeanne, je croyais que ton frère ne savait pas nager.
– Oui, c'est vrai. Et alors?
– Mais qu'est-ce qu'il fait?
– Ben ... il me regarde, quoi!

– Oui, je voudrais bien partir en vacances avec toi, mais l'année prochaine je passe mon bac, alors je n'ai pas le temps de m'amuser.
– Mais Amélie, tu as bien le temps de prendre deux semaines de vacances, quand même.
– Euh ... non ... euh ... non vraiment, je ne crois pas.

8 Nous avons passé des vacances super. Nous avons trouvé un camping à deux cents mètres de la mer. C'était formidable.

9 – Hier soir, j'ai fait une boum chez moi.
– Et tes parents, qu'est-ce qu'ils ont dit?
– Ils sont allés voir ma grand-mère qui est malade.

10 Pour être médecin, il faut faire plusieurs années d'études, alors c'est ce que je vais faire, j'espère.

11 J'ai choisi la filière maths-sciences, parce que je ne suis pas forte en langues.

12 – On a eu pas mal de problèmes en vacances, tu sais?
– Comment ça?
– Ben, d'abord l'hôtel n'a pas trouvé ma réservation, alors ils nous ont donné une chambre au troisième et l'autre au cinquième. Mais en plus, l'ascenseur ne marchait pas. Je me suis plaint, naturellement, mais sans succès – et il n'était pas question de changer d'hôtel. Tous les hôtels de Nice étaient complets. Alors, nous sommes tous en forme maintenant, je t'assure.
– Alors, t'as pas passé de bonnes vacances?
– Oh si, quand même. Il a fait très beau, et le restaurant de l'hôtel était vraiment extra!

Answers

1 B

2 B

3 i C; ii A; iii D; iv F

4 C

5 A + C

6 ~~Dupuis~~ Dupond; ~~hôtel de ville~~ office du tourisme; ~~6h15~~ 16h15

7 égoïste J   sérieuse A

8 près de la mer/plage OR (à) 200m de la mer/plage

9 (allés) chez grand-mère/à la maison de grand-mère/allés visiter grand-mère.

10 Il veut/désire/va être médecin.

11 Elle est forte en maths OR Elle n'est pas forte dans les autres matières/en langues.

12 A Hotel had lost booking + Rooms a long way apart/on different floors + lift not working (ANY TWO)
   B Hotel(s) full
   C Everyone got fit
   D (i) enjoyed it/had a good time
      (ii) good food/restaurant + good weather

4 Here you need to eliminate the possibilities as you hear extra information. For example, you can eliminate **D** when you hear *Je n'aime pas trop voyager*.

5 In quite a long utterance, it's not easy to keep both sets of prices in your head, and to pick out a very short word – *russe* – and link it with *étranger*.

6 The time could be difficult (*six/seize*).

A Grade C candidate would probably not have dropped any marks so far.

7 These are both quite hard gist items, with colloquial expressions, hesitations, etc. to make them more difficult. In addition, you never hear on the CD the words in the question, nor even single words which have the same meaning.

8 You need to be careful with your expression in French. *Sur la plage*, for example, would not be correct.

9 Again, *grand-mère* alone would not do; you have to be more precise.

A Grade B candidate would only have dropped one or possibly two marks so far.

10–11 You have to produce meaningful sentences which answer the questions – but minor spelling errors won't make any difference to the mark.

12 A There are many different ways of expressing these ideas – it's the facts which matter, not the exact words used.

B Like **A**, these are fairly straightforward factual answers, but you have to identify them within quite a long conversation. However, the questions will almost always come in the same order that you hear the information – except of course when it's a gist question.

C Here you have to make the link between the lift not working and the result.

D (i) You have to connect the question with the answer (and understand si meaning 'yes' after a negative question) to get the answer.

(ii) Two more factual details, but there is some colloquial French (extra) to understand.

An A∗ candidate would probably score very close to full marks – say at least 22/23 out of 25.

ANSWERS AND TRANSCRIPTS
FOR QUESTIONS TO TRY

Unit 15: Exam practice Speaking (pages 104–7)

🥖 Role-plays

Transcripts for sample student's answers

1 *Teacher:* Oui, mademoiselle?
Student: Je voudrais jouer au tennis.
Teacher: Vous êtes combien?
Student: Il y a quatre personnes.
Teacher: D'accord.
Student: C'est combien?
Teacher: Vous voulez jouer combien de temps?
Student: Deux heures.
Teacher: Alors, c'est quatre euros soixante par personne.

Examiner's comments
Although sometimes it is possible at this level to answer with a single word and gain full marks (this candidate could just have said 'quatre' for her second utterance), sometimes you have to say more than that. For instance, the candidate's first utterance needs to be a sentence – 'tennis' on its own would not be enough – and you almost always need a verb to ask a question.

2 *Teacher:* Bonjour monsieur. Vous désirez?
Student: Je voudrais une limonade.
Teacher: Vous voulez quelque chose à manger?
Student: Un sandwich au jambon, s'il vous plaît.
Teacher: Voilà monsieur.
Student: Où est le téléphone?
Teacher: Au premier étage.
Student: Merci.
Teacher: De rien.

Examiner's comments
When you have a choice of items, make sure you choose one you are absolutely sure you know in French. Also make sure you are familiar with the meanings of any symbols used by your examining group.

3 *Teacher:* Où est-ce que tu travailles?
Student: Je travaille dans un supermarché.
Teacher: Quelles sont tes heures de travail?
Student: De cinq heures à neuf heures.
Teacher: Tu travailles quel jour?
Student: Lundi.
Teacher: Et tu gagnes combien de l'heure?
Student: Quatre livres.

4 *Teacher:* Oui, monsieur? Je peux vous aider?
Student: J'ai perdu ma valise.
Teacher: Vous pouvez décrire la valise?
Student: Elle est petite et noire.
Teacher: Où l'avez-vous perdu, monsieur?
Student: Je l'ai laissé dans un taxi.
Teacher: Vous êtes en France jusqu'à quand?
Student: Je rentre en Angleterre mardi prochain.

5 *Teacher:* Oui, mademoiselle?
Student: Je voudrais une chambre avec douche, s'il vous plaît.
Teacher: C'est pour combien de personnes?
Student: C'est pour une personne.
Teacher: Vous restez combien de temps?
Student: C'est pour une nuit.
Teacher: Chambre numéro onze.
Student: Le petit déjeuner est à quelle heure?
Teacher: De sept heures et demie à neuf heures.

6 *Teacher:* Alors, qu'est-ce que tu as fait en Normandie?
Student: D'abord, nous sommes allés dans un petit bar pour
prendre le petit déjeuner. Nous avons mangé des
croissants, et moi, j'ai pris du chocolat chaud.
Teacher: C'était bon?
Student: Oui, c'était excellent. Après, puisqu'il faisait assez froid,
nous avons fait des courses.
Teacher: Qu'est-ce que tu as acheté?
Student: J'ai acheté des souvenirs. Pour mon père, j'ai acheté des
chocolats, et pour ma mère j'ai choisi du parfum.
Teacher: Elle l'a aimé?

ANSWERS AND TRANSCRIPTS
FOR QUESTIONS TO TRY

Student:	Oh oui, elle adore le parfum. J'ai aussi acheté des cadeaux pour mes amies. J'ai dépensé vingt-trois euros.
Teacher:	Et qu'est-ce que tu as fait d'autre?
Student:	Nous sommes allés à la cathédrale, et nous avons visité le musée.
Teacher:	C'était intéressant?
Student:	Non, je n'aime pas beaucoup les musées, alors j'ai trouvé ça un peu ennuyeux.
Teacher:	Et l'après-midi?
Student:	Nous sommes allés à la plage, où nous avons mangé un pique-nique, et nous avons joué au volley. Le soir, nous avons dîné au restaurant, puis nous sommes allés en discothèque. Nous nous sommes couchés très tard.
Teacher:	Merci, c'était très intéressant.

Examiner's comments

This is a different sort of role-play, and most of the comments are equally appropriate to the Presentation or the General Conversation. This has to be a narrative in the past, and the candidate takes full advantage to include a variety of different kinds of past tense, using *être*, *avoir* and a reflexive verb. He adds in a lot of extra details, but is careful to leave nothing out. He answers the teacher's questions well and without hesitation.

 7

Teacher:	Bonjour monsieur. Qu'est-ce que vous avez?
Student:	J'ai de la fièvre, et j'ai mal à l'estomac.
Teacher:	Vous êtes malade depuis quand?
Student:	Ça a commencé hier soir.
Teacher:	Et qu'est-ce que vous avez fait hier?
Student:	Je suis allé en ville faire des courses.
Teacher:	Quand est-ce que vous rentrez chez vous?
Student:	Est-ce que je pourrai partir demain?
Teacher:	Oui, sans problème.

Examiner's comments

If the task contains a plural (like here: *symptômes*) make sure you give at least two. Remember, if the task ends in a **?** you need to **ask** a question. For the unprepared utterance, you need to listen especially carefully to what the teacher says – particularly when it's very hard to predict.

 8

Teacher:	Pourquoi est-ce que vous voulez travailler en France?
Student:	Je voudrais perfectionner mon français.
Teacher:	Qu'est-ce que vous avez déjà fait comme travail?
Student:	J'ai travaillé dans un petit magasin.
Teacher:	Ah bon!
Student:	Je vais commencer et finir à quelle heure?
Teacher:	Les heures sont de 6 heures à minuit, du mardi au samedi. Vous pouvez commencer quand?
Student:	Je peux commencer la semaine prochaine.

Teacher:	Excellent.
Student:	Je gagnerai combien?
Teacher:	Sept cents euros par semaine.

> **Examiner's comments**
>
> The teacher's use of the past in the second question should prompt you to use the past in your answer. If you don't know how to put *'heures de travail'* into your answer, say something simpler, but equally good.

✎ Presentation and Discussion

Transcript for sample student's Presentation

| Teacher: | Alors, tu vas me parler de ta famille, n'est-ce pas? |
| Student: | Oui. J'ai une assez grande famille. J'ai deux frères et une sœur, et j'ai aussi deux demi-frères, car mes parents sont divorcés, et mon père s'est remarié. J'habite avec ma mère et mes frères et sœur dans une petite maison. Mes frères partagent une chambre, et moi, je dois partager une chambre avec ma sœur. D'habitude, ça va, car nous nous entendons assez bien. Elle s'appelle Louise, et elle a deux ans de moins que moi. Nous nous parlons de tout – de l'école, des garçons, du cinéma, de la musique. Heureusement, nous avons les mêmes goûts – nous aimons les mêmes vêtements. Louise est assez grande pour son âge, alors elle m'emprunte mes robes, et moi, je fais pareil. Quelquefois c'est difficile, parce que j'ai des examens, et elle n'en a pas, mais normalement elle me laisse la chambre, et elle va écouter ses disques dans le salon. Après les examens, on va passer quinze jours ensemble à Londres, chez ma tante.

Mes frères, par contre, ne sont pas sympa. Ils ont onze ans – ce sont des jumeaux – et ils sont vraiment casse-pieds. Ils sont stupides et égoïstes. Quelquefois, ma mère doit nous séparer. La semaine dernière, par exemple, Tony a pris un de mes cahiers pour écrire une lettre. C'était mon cahier d'histoire, et j'avais un examen deux jours après. Heureusement, Louise l'a vu, et elle me l'a rendu. |
Teacher:	Tu t'entends bien avec ta mère?
Student:	Oui. Elle est très sympa. Elle travaille dans une banque, et elle est souvent fatiguée, mais si j'ai un problème elle m'écoute toujours.
Teacher:	Et ton père?
Student:	Oh, ça va. Je vois mon père presque tous les week-ends, et on va au cinéma. Mais ma sœur, elle, ne s'entend pas du tout avec lui. Quelquefois elle refuse de venir avec moi quand je vais le voir.
Teacher:	Merci.

🥖 General Conversation

Transcript for sample teacher's questions

- Où habites-tu?
- Qu'est-ce que tu as fait pour aider à la maison la semaine dernière?
- Parle-moi de ta chambre.
- Qu'est-ce que tu vas faire ce week-end?
- Quels sont tes loisirs?
- Qu'est-ce que tu as fait hier soir?
- Parle-moi de ton collège.
- Qu'est-ce que tu vas faire l'année prochaine?
- Tu as déjà choisi un métier?

Transcript for sample Conversation

Teacher: Où habites-tu?

Student: J'habite à Portsmouth, dans le sud de l'Angleterre. J'habite dans une grande maison près du centre-ville. Il y a quatre chambres et un grand jardin. C'est une assez vieille maison, alors les pièces sont grandes, mais en hiver on a toujours froid, car on n'a pas le chauffage central.

Teacher: Qu'est-ce que tu as fait pour aider à la maison la semaine dernière?

Student: Samedi j'ai lavé la voiture de mon père. J'ai aussi fait un peu de jardinage. J'ai fait la vaisselle tous les jours, et mardi j'ai préparé le repas du soir, car ma mère est sortie. J'ai aussi rangé et nettoyé ma chambre.

Teacher: Parle-moi de ta chambre.

Student: Elle est assez petite. Il y a juste la place pour mon lit, une armoire, et la table où je fais mes devoirs. J'adore ma chambre. Les murs sont bleus, et les rideaux sont jaunes. Je l'ai décorée moi-même.

Teacher: Qu'est-ce que tu vas faire ce week-end?

Student: Samedi après-midi, je vais aller en ville avec mes copines.

Nous allons faire des courses. Je vais m'acheter une jupe et peut-être un pull. Après, nous irons au café pour retrouver Paul et John, et le soir nous allons à une boum. Dimanche, je ferai la grasse matinée jusqu'à onze heures. L'après-midi, j'irai voir ma grand-mère, qui habite à la campagne.

Teacher: Quels sont tes loisirs?

Student: J'aime le sport – je joue souvent au tennis et au volley. J'adore aussi la lecture. Je préfère les romans policiers, mais je lis aussi des magazines. Mais ma passion, c'est la natation. Je vais à la piscine au moins deux fois par semaine, et en vacances, je passe tout mon temps à me baigner. Ce que je n'aime pas beaucoup, c'est regarder la télé. Je trouve ça ennuyeux.

Teacher: Qu'est-ce que tu as fait hier soir?

Student: Il y avait un film à la télé que je voulais voir, mais il n'était pas très bon, alors je me suis couchée de bonne heure.

Teacher: Parle-moi de ton collège.

Student: Il est grand. Il y a mille cent élèves et soixante profs. Ce n'est pas mal comme collège. Je trouve les cours assez intéressants, et les profs sont sympa. En plus, j'ai beaucoup d'amis au collège.

Teacher: Qu'est-ce que tu vas faire l'année prochaine?

Student: Je crois que je vais retourner au collège pour continuer mes études, mais ça dépend des résultats de mes examens. Si c'est possible, je voudrais étudier les sciences et les maths.

Teacher: Tu as déjà choisi un métier?

Student: Non. J'avais pensé devenir médecin, mais maintenant je ne sais plus. Je crois que je voudrais travailler dans l'informatique – mais on verra. D'abord, il faut réussir aux examens, puis je voudrais aller à l'université.

Examiner's comments

This is an example of what can be done. No one candidate ever (or anyway very rarely) performs like this, but a good candidate can produce some sections of this quality. It's not so much the individual bits which make it so good – you will find all the phrases and vocabulary in the first 13 units of this book – it's the way they're put together, and particularly the way the candidate never stops at the minimum answer, but always goes on to add extra details, give opinions and examples, and respond fluently and naturally. Of course, there is a wide variety of tenses and some complex structures such as *qui* and *que* clauses.

If you don't think you can sustain this sort of performance, don't worry. This candidate would have scored an A* with plenty to spare – what you should do is to make sure that at least one or two of your answers are of this sort of length and complexity. If you do that, you could be well on the way to an A* yourself!

ANSWERS AND TRANSCRIPTS
FOR QUESTIONS TO TRY

Unit 16: Exam practice
Reading (pages 119–23)

Answers

1 B [1]

> **Examiner's comments**
> *Gare routière* is, of course, a bus station.

2 **A** children [1 mark] from 3 to 13 [1 mark] [2]
B Mondays [1]
C touch (the animals) [1]

> **Examiner's comments**
> Make sure you give all the information required. In **A**, 'children' and the age-range are both important.

3 Chambre E; Cuisine F; Salon B; Jardin A; Salle de bains C; Salle à manger D [6]

4 **A** mauvais
B contente
C dans un village
D bien dormir [4]

> **Examiner's comments**
> It's useful to realise that there are four questions and four paragraphs.
>
> **A** is fairly clear, since Amélie makes three separate complaints about the journey.
> **B** too is quite clearly complimentary.
> **C** is a little more difficult, since traffic noise might lead you to think of a town, but *loin des autres maisons* combined with traffic noise can only fit *dans un village*.
> **D** Amélie is clearly more concerned with getting a good night's sleep than with going to the beach!

5

	Julie	Alexandre	Aurélie
Je suis fils/fille unique.		✔	
Je m'entends bien avec ma sœur.			✔
J'ai une assez grande famille.	✔		

[3]

> **Examiner's comments**
> When you have to compare a number of passages, as here, there is always rather more work to do, but it can be done fairly quickly. You can eliminate Julie and Aurélie from being only children, as they both mention brothers and/or sisters. If Alexandre is an only child, the second and third statements can't apply to him. Aurélie talks a lot about her sister, while Julie has three brothers and two sisters. You need to do this sort of calculation quite quickly at this stage.

6 A ✓; C ✓; E ✓ [3]

> **Examiner's comments**
> **A** The quality of Beso's paintings is the subject of the article.
> **B** Is wrong. He has been painting **since** he was 4.
> **C** You need to spot the negative here. *Beso **n'est pas** d'une famille riche.*
> **D** Is wrong. The exhibition (*exposition*) is in London, but Beso **comes** from Georgia.
> **E** This depends on putting together the last two sentences of the passage: 'That's what he paints.'

7 1 F; **2** A; **3** D; **4** B [4]

> **Examiner's comments**
> To begin with the easy options, only **E** and **F** could follow 1, and *Europe* is too limited for what Martine says. Number 4 can't logically be followed by an infinitive, which leaves **B** as the best answer, since **C** is not true. You can then start to work out answers for **2** and **3** – not too hard when you've eliminated some of the possibilities already.

8 **A** Olivier; **B** Sandrine; **C** Tiphaine; **D** Sandrine [4]

> **Examiner's comments**
> Don't forget, these questions all relate to what the people actually say. Make sure you understand the questions first, then go through the text until you find someone who definitely fits.

9 **A** They have become illegal/they have had to hide [1]
   B The police broke in/used force/used tear-gas [1]
   C People are afraid/
     People think immigrants cause unemployment/
     People think immigrants are responsible for street violence
       ANY ONE [1]
   D Immigrants are the victims/
     Immigrants suffer most from unemployment/
     Immigrants suffer most from street violence
       ANY ONE [1]
   E Sympathetic to (problems of) immigrants [1]

> **Examiner's comments**
> Each of these questions requires you to understand the gist of a section of the article. Once you have decided where to look for the answer, the task becomes quite a lot easier. Remember, you are really being asked for a summary here, so you need to do more than just translate one or two details. In addition, the last question requires you to give an impression of the overall tone of the whole passage, not just to concentrate on one paragraph.

[Total: 34 marks]

ANSWERS AND TRANSCRIPTS
FOR QUESTIONS TO TRY

Unit 17: Exam practice
Writing (pages 132–6)

FOUNDATION

These questions are aimed at G/F/E candidates. To get a Grade E, you would need to communicate all or almost all the ideas to a sympathetic French speaker who understands no English.

Sample student's answers

1

1	serviette
2	portable
3	appareil photo
4	valise
5	lunettes de soleil
6	argent
7	maillot de bain
8	portefeuille

Examiner's comments

You could have chosen to use the other words: *casquette*; *billets*; *sandales*; *passeport*; *sac à main*. The only guidance is 'Choose words you are sure of, and if possible, words you know you can spell right'. Spelling mistakes may not cost you the mark if the meaning is still clear, but if you end up with a different French word (e.g. *agent* instead of *argent*), you won't get the mark.

2

A Hélène	prend	l'	autobus .
B Hélène	va	en	ville .
C Elle	achète	une	jupe .
D Elle	rentre	à la	maison .
E Elle	fait	ses	devoirs .

Examiner's comments

This is not just a vocabulary exercise. It also requires you to handle verbs accurately. The verbs here are all very common. You should learn all their parts in the present tense, but make sure you know the *je* and *il/elle* forms – these are the ones you are certain to need.

3

> J'ai un frère et deux sœurs.
> Nous avons un chien et un poisson rouge.
> Mon père travaille dans un bureau.
> Ma maison est grande et moderne.
> Ma mère est sympa et calme.

FOUNDATION/HIGHER

These questions are aimed at Grade D/C candidates. As well as requiring longer answers, you will only gain the higher marks if you express some personal opinions, and refer to past, present and future events (the questions are designed to force you to do this!).

Sample student's answers

4

> Mes vacances étaient super. Je suis allée à la plage tous les jours et j'ai joué au volley. Le soir, j'ai dansé dans une boîte.
>
> L'année prochaine, je vais étudier les maths et les sciences, parce que je voudrais être médecin. Ma matière préférée, c'est la chimie. Je déteste la géographie.
>
> Le week-end, je vais en ville avec mes copines. J'adore faire les courses. Puis nous allons au café pour rencontrer nos petits amis.

ANSWERS AND TRANSCRIPTS FOR QUESTIONS TO TRY

5

(Le week-end) Je travaille dans un (petit) restaurant (au centre-ville). Je fais la vaisselle (et j'aide à préparer les repas).

Je travaille (le vendredi et le samedi) de six heures à onze heures.

Je reçois quatre livres de l'heure. (Ce n'est pas beaucoup.)

La semaine dernière, j'ai acheté des cd (car j'aime bien la musique pop, surtout le rap) (et je suis allé au cinéma).

J'aime le travail (mais c'est très fatigant).

A l'avenir je ne vais pas faire cette sorte de travail (parce que ce n'est pas assez bien payé).

(Alors) Je vais devenir professeur (de français).

Examiner's comments

Although there are no errors, this is a poor answer in a number of ways (indicated by the fact that there are only 48 words). There are no descriptions and only one opinion. The brackets give you some ideas of where you could extend your answer.

NB In this task, there is only one question aimed at the past, and one at the future. This means that if you fail to complete either of those two tasks, you won't have fulfilled the requirements for Grade C, and your marks will be greatly reduced. Make sure that you complete **all** the tasks, and make your past and future references accurate enough to be understood.

6

J'attends avec impatience ma visite chez toi en France. Pendant mon séjour, est-ce qu'on pourra aller nager dans le lac? Aussi, je voudrais bien jouer au tennis avec toi et ta famille.

Ici en Angleterre, je vais souvent à la piscine. D'habitude, il fait trop froid pour nager en plein air, même en été!

Je déteste faire des promenades à pied, mais mes parents adorent ça! Tous les dimanches, nous faisons au moins dix kilomètres. J'ai mal aux pieds!

Le week-end dernier, je suis allée à un parc d'attractions avec des copines. C'était super. Je me suis bien amusée.

Examiner's comments

There really is nothing missing from this answer. It has the compulsory references to past (three verbs), present and future (two references), a number of personal opinions, and plenty of extra detail. Here are some of the particularly 'good' bits: it's worth trying to remember at least some of them to use in your own answers:

- *J'attends avec impatience*
- *chez toi*
- *pendant mon séjour*
- *est-ce qu'on pourra*
- *tous les dimanches*

and also the use of little words/phrases which make the piece flow:

- *aussi*
- *ici*
- *souvent*
- *d'habitude*
- *même*
- *au moins*

HIGHER

Sample student's answers

7

L'homme est **responsable** de toute la pollution. L'industrie a pollué **l'atmosphère**, ce qui provoque beaucoup de maladies. Nous avons aussi pollué les mers et les rivières avec nos **déchets**.

Mais à mon avis, **le problème le plus important**, c'est la voiture. Si nous continuons à utiliser les voitures comme nous le faisons en ce moment, nous détruirons notre planète. Car **les gaz d'échappement** sont la cause principale du **réchauffement de la terre**, et si le climat change, la vie deviendra impossible. En tout cas, nous ne pouvons pas continuer à consommer tant d'essence, car **le pétrole** sera bientôt **épuisé**.

Pour réduire ce problème, nous pouvons aller au collège à pied ou en vélo, au lieu d'y aller avec maman en voiture. Nous devons aussi encourager nos parents à utiliser plus souvent **les transports en commun**.

Pour **conserver les ressources naturelles**, nous devons éteindre la lumière quand nous quittons une pièce, et essayer de recycler le plus souvent possible les bouteilles, le papier et les métaux.

Examiner's comments

This area of 'world issues', especially the environment, can seem to be the most difficult to write about. However, once you have learnt a certain amount of 'technical' vocabulary, the language you need is not that much more complex than for any other Higher Tier topic. With words/phrases such as the ones in bold above, you can handle any 'environmental' theme. At this level, though, you do need to use some more complex sentences and constructions: *ce qui...* in the first paragraph; two *si* clauses in the second, as well as a variety of future tenses; a range of infinitive constructions throughout (after *devoir, pouvoir, continuer à, encourager à, essayer de, pour* and *au lieu de*).

8

Nous étions cinq dans la voiture de mon copain André. Après **à peu près** huit heures de route, nous sommes enfin arrivés.

Le camping était situé près d'une rivière, et **on nous a donné** un emplacement **au bord de l'eau**. Nous avons **décidé de dresser** la tente tout de suite, car le ciel était devenu **tout noir**, et il commençait à pleuvoir.

Puis le vent a commencé à souffler fort. La tente s'est envolée, et **toutes nos affaires** sont tombées dans la rivière. Une famille **nous a invités** à passer la nuit dans leur caravane, mais à trois heures du matin, **on nous a réveillés**. Il **fallait** évacuer le camping, **à cause des** inondations.

Alors, nous sommes rentrés chez nous **le lendemain**, et moi, j'ai dû passer trois jours au lit, car j'étais enrhumé.

Je voudrais bien faire du camping **encore une fois**, mais **la prochaine fois** je ne choisirais pas un camping près d'une rivière.

Examiner's comments

This piece clearly fulfils all the criteria to be awarded the very highest marks. It is accurate and reads fluently, and there are full descriptions and accounts. Although much of the vocabulary is straightforward, it is always appropriate to the task, and there is a variety of structures and tenses, good use of pronouns and agreements, especially of past participles.

9

Quand je suis arrivée chez Charlotte, ma correspondante **belge**, j'étais tout de suite **déçue**. Elle habitait une **petite** maison **sombre** dans un village **perdu** – il n'y avait **même pas** de bar! **En plus** j'ai dû partager la chambre de Charlotte, **qui** n'était pas **plus grande** que **la mienne** – **que** j'ai pour moi **toute seule**.

Charlotte se disputait **tout le temps** avec sa mère et sa sœur – son père **était parti** travailler six mois aux Etats-Unis. Ce n'était pas une famille heureuse **comme chez moi**.

Pour sortir, nous avons fait beaucoup de promenades dans les bois, **même s'il pleuvait**. Nous ne sommes pas allées en ville, et **je n'ai pas pu** acheter de cadeaux pour mes parents.

Ça m'a fait **tellement** plaisir de retrouver ma famille normale, même mon petit frère, **qui** est **si casse-pieds. Je ne crois pas que** j'inviterai Charlotte à venir chez moi, car nous n'avons pas du tout les mêmes intérêts.

Examiner's comments

This piece contains many good elements: there are a lot of adjectives, with agreements where necessary, and excellent use of link words to make the sentences longer and more interesting. The use of subordinate clauses (*qui* and *que*) is particularly impressive.

Try to learn the highlighted words/phrases in the last three pieces, and next time you are given a letter or an account to write, see how many of them would be appropriate to the title.

ANSWERS AND TRANSCRIPTS
FOR QUESTIONS TO TRY

INDEX

accommodation 65, 67
accounts (written style) 129
adjectives 1, 22, 45
   comparative 38
   demonstrative 64
   indefinite 75-6
   intensifiers 137-8
   possessive 22
   Reading Test 111
   superlative 63
adverbs 45
   comparative 38, 45
   indefinite 75-6
   intensifiers 137-8
advertisements 59-62, 112, 115
age 19
air transport 46, 47, 48
alphabet 80, 97
animals 20, 36
announcements 86
annual holidays 23
apologies 15
articles (grammar) 17
articles (written style) 128
avoir 12, 13

body parts 13
breakdown (car) 48

calendar 1, 5
   annual holidays 23
camping 65
cars 46, 47, 48
ce qui/ce que 34
chemists 15
cinema 29, 30
clothes 40, 41, 42
commands 1, 6
communication 59-62
comparisons 37, 38, 45, 63
complaints 15
conditional perfect tense 144
conditional tense 39
conjunctions 140
consonants 81, 96
conversations 102-3, 107
cooking 67
countries 71
   comparisons 37
   flags 20
   United Kingdom 40
countryside 35, 37
crockery 14
cutlery 14

daily routine 1, 7
dates 5, 43
   annual holidays 23

definite articles 17
demonstrative adjectives 64
demonstrative pronouns 64
depuis 6
descriptions 19, 20, 22, 62, 102-3
dialogues 85
diet 15
directions 46, 48
discussions 100-101, 107
dishes 14, 15, 67
dress 40, 41, 42
driving 46, 47, 48

education 53, 55 (*see also* school)
emphatic pronouns 34
employment 53-5
   advertising 59-62
en (pronoun) 33
energy sources 73
entertainment 23-5, 29-31
environment 72-3
excursions 67
eye colour 20

family 9, 19, 21
farm animals 36
ferries 46, 47
films 29
finding the way 46
fitness 13, 15
flags (national) 20
food 14, 15, 67
foreign countries 71
   comparisons 37
   flags 20
foreign languages 71
fractions 44
free time 23-5, 29-31
friends 21
furniture 8
further education 53, 55
future perfect tense 143
future tense 38-9

games 23, 24, 25
gender 16
getting around 46-8
global problems 72-3
greetings 30

hairstyles 19
health 13, 15
hobbies 23, 24, 25
holidays 23, 25, 65, 67
home life 7-9
home town 35, 37
hotels 65, 67
houses 7

housework 7
how long for 6
human body 13

il y a 70
illness 13, 15
imperative 1, 6
imperfect tense 69
impersonal verbs 143
indefinite adjectives, adverbs and
   pronouns 75-6
indefinite articles 17
infinitive 26
intensifiers 137-8
interviews 61
introductions 29
irregular verbs
   common verbs 12, 140-43
   er verbs 10
   future tense 39

jobs 53-5
   advertisements 59-62

language patterns 81, 111
languages 71
leisure 23-5, 29-31
lessons 1, 2, 3
letters (written style) 112, 116, 128
letters of the alphabet 80, 97
Listening Test 77-91
local environment 35, 37

magazines 112, 115
materials 42
meals 7
measurement 40, 44, 46
media 59-62, 112, 115
meetings 29-30
menus 14
money 23, 25, 40, 42
monologues 85
months 1, 5
motoring 46, 47, 48
multiple-choice questions 87-8, 117-18

nationalities 20
negatives 25, 57-8, 81
negotiating 15
newspapers 112, 115
notices 115
nouns 16
   Reading Test 111
numbers 43-4, 80

object pronouns 32-3
offices 62
opinions 9, 21, 30, 83-4, 102, 112

parts of the body 13
passive 58
past historic tense 144
past participle 27
past tenses *see* imperfect tense;
   perfect tense; pluperfect tense
pastimes 23-5
percentages 43
perfect tense 27-8
personal characteristics 62
personal relationships 29-30
pluperfect tense 69-70
plurals 16, 22
possessive adjectives 22
possessive pronouns 137
prepositions 139-40
present participle 18
present tense 10-11
presentations 100-101, 107
prices 23, 40, 42
pronouns
   ce qui/ce que 34
   demonstrative 64
   emphatic 34
   en 33
   indefinite 75-6
   object 32-3
   order 34, 138
   possessive 137
   qui/que 33
   relative 75, 138-9
   subject 32
   y 33
pronunciation 95-7
public announcements 86
public events 60
public services 40, 42

quantity 40, 44, 46
questions 1, 50-51
qui/que (pronoun) 33

radio 9
Reading Test 108-23
recipes 67

recorded messages 86
reflexive verbs 11, 28, 70
relative pronouns 75, 138-9
restaurants 14, 15
role-plays 98-9, 104-7
rooms 7

school 53
   daily routine 1
   subjects 1, 2, 3
   types of school 3
   year groups 3
seasons 35
self (description) 19-21
shopping 40, 42
shops 35, 40, 42
signs 46, 48
skimming (reading) 114
small ads 60
social activities 29-30
Speaking Test 92-107
special occasions 23, 60
sport 24, 25
stars (media, music, sport) 71, 72
subject pronouns 32
subjunctive 144-5
superlative 63

telephone conversations 59, 86
telephone numbers 44, 59
television 9
theatre 30
time 1, 5-6, 46
times of day 2
tourism 65, 67
towns 35, 37, 46, 67
training 53, 55
trains 46, 47, 48
transport 46-8
travel 46-8, 67, 71

vehicles 46-8
venir de + infinitive 70
verbs
   conditional perfect tense 144

   conditional tense 39
   er verbs 10, 145-7
   future perfect tense 143
   future tense 38-9
   imperative 1, 6
   imperfect tense 69
   impersonal verbs 143
   infinitive 26
   ir verbs 11, 147
   irregular verbs 10, 12, 39, 140-43
   negatives 25, 57-8, 81
   passive 58
   past historic tense 144
   past participle 27
   perfect tense 27-8
   pluperfect tense 69-70
   present participle 18
   present tense 10-11
   pronunciation 97
   re verbs 11, 147
   Reading Test 110-11
   reflexive verbs 11, 28, 70
   subjunctive 144-5
   use of tenses 102
vocabulary 109-10
vowels 95

weather 35, 37
weights and measures 40, 44, 46
word patterns 81, 111
word separation 82
work 53-5
   communication 59-62
world
   countries 71
   comparisons 37
   flags 20
   global problems 72-3
Writing Test 124-36

y (pronoun) 33
yourself (description) 19-21
youth hostels 65